C000296503

CARLO COLOMBO

CARLO COLOMBO

Industrial Design

edited by Maria Vittoria Capitanucci

Rizzoli
NEW YORK

New York Paris London Milan

strial Design

4

Industrial De

"The cultural component of the project
is the essence capable of distinguishing a copy
from the reinterpretation of the signs from the past.

"Respect for the rules is essential to a designer's growth.
The concepts of memory, irony, and function are crucial
ingredients in the success of a project. I have always
tried to treasure these 'rules' which I see as objects
stimulating reflection and growth."

CONTENTS

4 Industrial Design
8 Preface Vittorio Sgarbi
12 Preface Flavio Manzoni
16 1990*2020
19 30 Years of Design

20 Works Selection

22 Europe

24 Opale
26 Cap Ferrat
28 Cap Martin Sunset
32 Milano 2015
34 Big Outdoor
36 Sveva
40 Butterfly
42 Zigo Zago
44 Edmond
46 Albume
50 Fluido
52 Eva
58 Atlantic
62 Amalia
64 Monaco
66 Royale
68 Slope
70 A-Round
72 Taylor
74 Sahrai 1
76 Sahrai 2
78 Tuba
80 Baia
82 Leiston
84 Twelve
86 Chloe
88 Sliver
90 Je Suis
92 Dunes
94 Elite
98 Knokke
102 Big Sveva
104 Lugano

106 Industrial Design

108 Asia

110 Jaipur
112 Charlotte
114 Amal
116 Sushi
118 Eclipse
120 Barrel
122 Aldia
130 Shirley
132 Koi
134 Oval Chair
136 L'Infini
138 Spaziotempo
140 Isabel
144 Cobra Chair
146 Ramsey
150 Ago
152 Town
154 Bali
156 Altea
158 Berenice
160 Drive
162 Swing

164 North America

166	Cocca
168	Newbridge
172	Berry
174	Hester
176	Park 1
178	Alison Outdoor
182	Happ
184	Sit 414
186	Trail
188	Rugby
190	Urban
192	Softwing
194	ISØLA
198	Thorne
200	Glo
204	Ramsey
206	Ettore Desk
208	Bemade
210	Bigger
212	Diana
214	Icon
216	Hermann
218	Jeremy

220 South America

222	Eddy
224	Larzia
226	Elisabeth
228	Bentley Outdoor
234	Mere
236	Gentleman
238	CCLight
240	Buxton
242	Harrow
244	Tiverton
246	Newent
248	Skyline
252	Domus
256	Styal Desk
260	Bampton
264	Zoe

266 Art Design Collection

270	784
274	Raspberry
278	Folio
282	Halfpipe
284	Ball
288	Fold
292	Lobster
296	Bullfrog

7

CARLO COLOMBO
30 years of design

Preface

by Vittorio Sgarbi

Carlo Colombo's armchair is a monument without a man. A throne without a king. The architect does not hold himself back. He prepares the ceremony and the ceremonial. And, if it is a baptism, the baptismal font too. What Giulio Cappellini says about him is a precise clue: "In the world of contemporary creativity, quite often leveled down by rigid market rules, Carlo is able to express himself without ever forgetting people's real dreams and needs." How can dreams be more real than needs? Of course, sofas like Cap Ferrat and Cap Martin Sunset are apparently simple and flexible, to adapt to different and variable situations. They are not for the people: they are for the few and sensitive. The Milano 2015 lamp, in dialogue with FontanaArte, is a gelid form that renders the Carrara marble luminous and transfigures it, making it coincide with the light. The armchair, in its original function, awaiting a body, takes on feminine and masculine forms. With another technique and other intentions, Gaetano Pesce transformed it into the soft, passive female body itself. Colombo responds with his Eva, nervous, athletic, and reactive. Whether it is a bathtub or a sofa, Colombo's form is always rounded or concave, elastic or convex. Colombo is never passive. His form is always active and taut even when it alludes to comfort, as in the Jaipur bed, supported by macro wooden weaves: they are alert, nervous, edgy forms, like the Sushi armchair. Colombo ennobles contemporaneity: he sees himself in the glowing washbasin with an elliptical outline, enlivened by LED lights; and light, not water, seems to be contained in Barrel, a pure, solid, and compact monolith with the soft curvature of a cask. Colombo rehabilitates the simplest volumes, assigning them to their primary functions. Geometry and rigor are found in different objects: in the table lamp, as in the storage unit that is divided into variously modular blocks, to be composed depending on the requirements of space. For Arflex, as for Flexform with Alison, for interiors and exteriors, Colombo conceives objects as engaged in guerrilla warfare with the prevailing need to furnish: hence Rugby, hence the competitive Urban. Colombo's furnishings are like the buildings of an ideal city, which he calls contemporary Island, and it responds to the laws of a new city that I have called Sgarbistan, for which Colombo has also conceived a throne, in a very limited edition. He wanted to go beyond the scheme of the industrial revolution and create something unique and exclusive. The form of the body overspreads hundreds of gilded aluminum bars. To the eye, it appears a golden throne, transforming and dominating every space. The throne awaits a king. And, in the same spirit, Colombo conceives the democratic chair for twenty ministers of a phantom government. Or for the G20 that has just ended. Fuksas's Nuvola is matched by Colombo's Ball. For the king and queen of a world of lobsters, far from unlikely, he has created the abnormal Lobsters. In each of these inventions, the design industry transfers its democratic origin into the aristocratic. Colombo, in limited numbers, rehabilitates craft traditions. He is ready for a new world. Now he is waiting for men and women to populate it.

Carlo Colombo and Vittorio Sgarbi at the Mediolanum headquarters in Padua
for an art-related event, November 2021.

Preface

by Flavio Manzoni

Carlo Colombo is undoubtedly one of the Italian designers best known worldwide. In addition to the esteem I feel for him, for his profession as architect and designer, I am bound to him by close ties of friendship. I have had the pleasure of meeting him on several occasions at the Ferrari Style Center, of which I have been director since 2010, and I find this friendship and esteem reciprocated by the deep admiration that Carlo displays for the Ferrari brand and the work that my team and I have been doing for some time now at Maranello. Over the years I have come to appreciate Carlo's culture, his sensibility, that unquenchable love for art that often shines through the nuances of the nonverbal language of his works.

A pupil of Achille Castiglioni, Colombo was the beneficiary of the tradition of the purest Italian design, receiving it directly from its founding fathers and becoming an heir to that "Italian style" made famous in the world by the now celebrated exhibition *Italy: The New Domestic Landscape*, held at MoMA in New York in 1972. On that occasion it was immediately clear that Italian design represented something deeper than a "style" in the common sense of the word: it was a "cultural approach to the project." After World War II, the Italian lexicon became sculptural and refined, moving beyond the philosophy and austere forms of the Modern Movement and developing an aesthetic of the product that was expressive and aware of the symbolic role that design plays in contemporary society. It was then that the conviction that our industrial production had attained an unmatched level of refinement became widespread internationally. The key to the success of the "Italian line" lies in a differentiated and pluralistic approach, which has nothing to do with a "style," as happened, for instance, with the "International Style" of functionalism or American styling in the thirties. G.K. Koenig maintained that "the great Italian discovery was a structural reasoning that canceled any prevailing stylistic label, as it was the linguistic communicative structures that commanded the forms of objects." According to this theory, the identity of the product arises from analysis of the function and the technologies applied, not from a preconceived stylistic idea such as to condition the forms. The variety of results derives from this honesty of purpose underlying the actual design, which still astonishes the world today. The years from 1955 to 1975 were decisive in the context of mass styling; they testify to notable changes that produced a radical transformation both of the environment and the meaning commonly attributed to the concept of style itself. Design began to play a fundamental role and the exuberance of the early postwar years was replaced by the growing refinement of the goods produced. In the sixties, which coincided with the period of the economic miracle, to attract the market of young people, the watchword was "novelty": for consumer goods the forms became fun, the colors bright. Technology advanced and its accessories evolved from functional forms to a smooth

"techno-chic." The new style made no concessions to the past; it represented contemporary society, dominated by consumerist exhibitionism. Marco Zanuso and Richard Sapper created absolute masterpieces for Brionvega. Mario Bellini designed the still very modern Divisumma for Olivetti. The Castiglioni brothers worked for Flos and Zanotta, as well as other companies. The Arco lamp, designed for Flos, probably represents the fundamental object of sixties design. This exceptional creative fervor and the eclecticism of our design have proved immensely influential in all fields. Carlo Colombo seems to be giving a sequel to those studies by proposing an original and contemporary interpretation of this type of aesthetic in his designer products. There are many interesting examples among his designs, such as the famous 784 armchair, for example, which I personally consider a masterpiece. There is a strong artistic concept behind this object, which from being functional becomes a work of art, without sacrificing factors such as ergonomics, comfort, and functionality. Between his approach to design and mine I could say that there are significant points of contact, especially in the conceptual phase. For both, if it is true that the form of an object must be wedded to the function, it is equally necessary for it to possess that flash of imagination, that insight that makes the object iconic, almost a modern and original archetype, without which the significance of design would be lacking. A designer object, I believe, must have an evocative purpose, a distinctive trait: a symbolic as well as functional value. The objects we produced, in addition to having a practical function, may be rich in symbolic, aesthetic, ethnic, and cultural values and are part of a communication system within society. The forms of objects convey more than aesthetic pleasure, by communicating through a nonverbal language, a metalanguage based on specific codes of communication. To put it in semiotic terms, in an object of design there are two quotients that must be in balance: the semantic quotient, which is linked to the function and is the purpose for which a given form was chosen, and the syntactic quotient, linked rather to the language of the form. We could define them as the functional quotient and the aesthetic quotient. Both of these factors, functional and aesthetic, are treated in detail by Colombo and justify the success of his projects. All his works are characterized by a clean and elegant line, as if linked by the same common thread. Smooth, polished surfaces emphasize his precise tactile choice: an evident preference for natural materials. Wood, metal, and stone alternate and complement one another, shaping objects of unexpected lightness with which Colombo often attains a refined and diverting effect of surprise, combining functionality, ergonomics, and the beauty of products with a bold creativity that is the legacy of the great masters of Italian design and the homage he pays to them.

Carlo Colombo and Flavio Manzoni (senior vice president of Ferrari Design), sharing
a passion for performance cars. At Maranello discussing design and approaches to
future developments. Alongside, on the circuit in Pavia.

"A passion for pure forms, elegance, and materials."
This is Carlo Colombo's aesthetic, earning him prolific collaborations with the most important historic Italian design companies.

1990*2020

A maverick in the international design world, acknowledged as one of the leading figures on the contemporary scene, yet completely independent, without a defined position within an enclave, movement, or trend, with an immense range of successful products designed for the most prestigious brands. As often happens with the most brilliant figures, Colombo's story is simple, as a builder of dreams for living, work, and leisure. It is a very low-profile story, sometimes rather restrained, never showy, but absolutely decisive, carefully thought out and fulfilled. After all, on Colombo's path we find a fascination with manufacturing, respect for those who produce, for those who accompany the process of design as a concept and a physical reality. Apart from being his professional occupation, design is his life story in which curiosity and passion are inseparably entwined with skill and competence. A story of passion, pragmatism, and feeling, of synergies with collaborators and companies, of inspiration that arises from encounters, travel, and, above all, from his passion for art. His is a curious gaze, as a lover of elegant and rarely striking gestures, a quality reserved for his most exclusive research on the boundaries of art and one-off pieces.

CARLO COLOMBO

Entering Carlo Colombo's design world is like embarking on a magnificent journey into an extremely personal and completely independent universe. His story is made up of creativity and passion for materials and the production process, with great respect for technical knowledge and craftsmanship. It is a story that is also formal and expressive research. A contemporary and sophisticated display, in which, as in an eighteenth-century court parade, elements of almost luxurious elegance alternate with severely minimalist pieces. His influences derive from the masters but also an innate freedom of design stemming from his encounters with places, his travels, the cities of the world, and landscapes as well as from ambience, memories, and allusions, but in the most unexpected fields. A traveler sui generis, with stated passions that enter the universe of his creativity. So it is for the world of automobiles, an aesthetic and transversal fascination that has never failed him, because it embodies that strength and energy inherent in speed, machinery, and continuous movement, aspects typical of Carlo Colombo's design as well as his character. A passionate car collector, he could hardly avoid introducing elements into his own design work that recall that specific universe in some wrap-around forms, ergonomic seating, constructional details, and high-tech materials worthy of the finest automotive engineering. So it is hardly surprising that he

has worked with well-known historical brands such as Bentley Home, for which he curated an especially sophisticated line of designer objects, including the magnificent Mere armchairs (2019), or the Royale sofa in carbon and leather (2017) or, again, the visionary Cobra chair (2017), the last two for Bugatti Home, with a line that differs from his work for Bentley by a sparer geometry in the elegant desks and office chairs. His passion for automobiles alternates with an interest in art, a central theme in the research conducted by this citizen of the world, with his heart at his debut in Brianza and his studies at the Politecnico di Milano, from which he graduated in 1993. Here he absorbed the postwar climate in Italy and seventies design culture together with the interdisciplinary nature of theoretical studies, with the good fortune to have the great Achille Castiglioni as his teacher. Hence a unique design path in which the two worlds of architecture and design are deliberately kept separate but never divided. Not surprisingly, in both fields his work reveals the strong influence of contemporary art, a constant reference in his creative choices, a common thread uniting and running through the professionalism of this "Janus facing two ways" with his irrepressible versatility, a collector of the great masters of the twentieth and twenty-first centuries.

30 years of design

This book is not meant to present a narrative structured around a timeline or types of products. Rather it is a journey through Carlo Colombo's vision and creativity, passing from one cultural position to another regardless of the time frame. Through large, almost dynamic images, sometimes graphically figurative, this account presents those subtle unifying threads connecting pieces and recounting places, influences, inspirations, stylistic and material research, passions, insights, and characters. The great cultural geographies into which the volume is divided, Europe, Asia, North America, and South America, are therefore Carlo Colombo's places, the regions of his experience and his creative and conceptual landmarks, but at the same time they are a structural device to guide the reader in rediscovering his inspiration and relating his products, lines, collections, and researches to an interdisciplinary universe that has transversal but also specific features in the various parts of the world. "Each continent has its own value and influence," argues Colombo, "and temporal discontinuity is necessary to avoid enclosing a piece in one time and place, so leaving open the endless potential for dialogue with creativity in the making." Opening each section, each of the four cultural geographies, is a symbolic image, a visual introduction to the narrative, in which words also acquire a compositional and graphic value. Each opening represents an image of life because it introduces a part of Carlo Combo's story that leads through the senses, that of his travels through cities and continents translated into his timeless design, suspended in time and space. It would have appealed to the great designers of the Milanese twentieth century, who provide Colombo with a frame of reference, together with the great masters on the international scene from the postwar period to the present, of which he is a passionate collector. The volume closes, naturally, with a section devoted to the universe of projects between art and design, comprising the series of striking and exclusive limited-edition pieces, conceived and produced over time by Colombo's passion and research.

1990*2020

WORKS
selection

EUROPE

The old continent for a classic but contemporary look.

Carlo Colombo certainly associates Europe with his Italian beginnings in the mid-nineties, with companies that already spoke an international language at the time. Those were the years when the centrality of Milan, the capital of design, was firmly established and the great Italian masters of the postwar period (Castiglioni, Magistretti) and those of the seventies (from Joe Colombo and Sottsass to Mendini passing through D'Urbino and Lomazzi), the two generations that started the great production of furniture designed and made in Italy, gave way to a new wave of designers from around the world. Companies were transformed into true forges of creativity and, apart from what they had in common, certainly the influences become intense, together with international fairs and travel. To Colombo, London meant the discovery of an elegant tradition combined with a visionary creativity. Think of the history of Bentley and, in a more sporting and aggressive gesture, the choices made in designing the French Bugatti. Britain also meant the encounter with that post-Archigram root later shared with the great "family"of Giulio Cappellini, as did Holland with its innovative language of forms and materials.

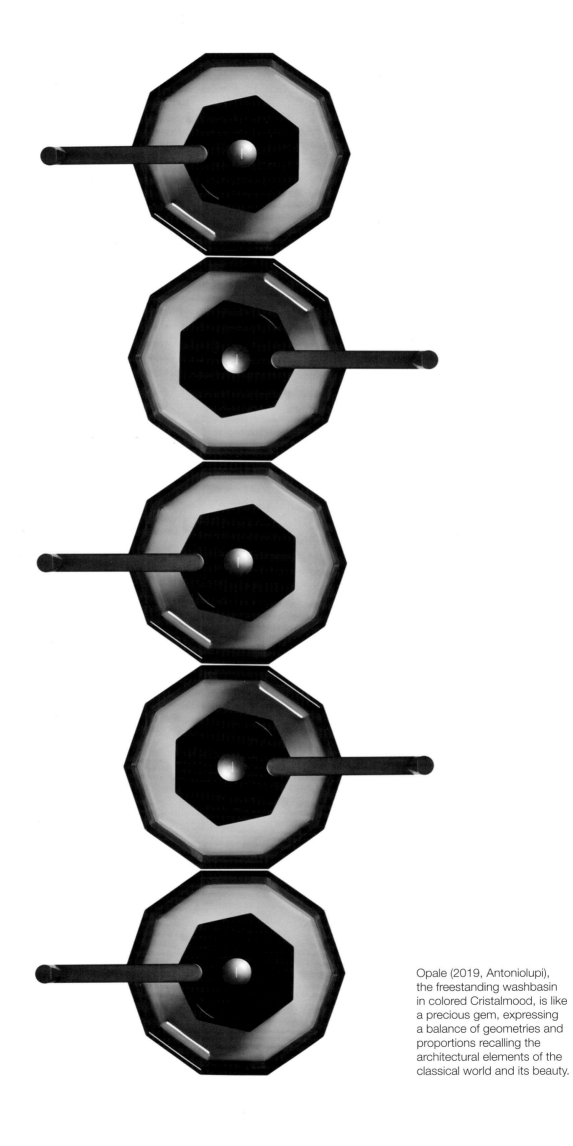

Opale (2019, Antoniolupi),
the freestanding washbasin
in colored Cristalmood, is like
a precious gem, expressing
a balance of geometries and
proportions recalling the
architectural elements of the
classical world and its beauty.

2020

Close ties with companies and friendships with a series of enlightened entrepreneurs are typical of Carlo Colombo's work. Giulio Cappellini said of him: "In the world of contemporary creativity, quite often leveled down by rigid market rules, Carlo is able to express himself without ever forgetting people's real dreams and needs."

The Cap Ferrat sofa (2020, Cappellini) embodies
the aesthetic values of a collection with an austere,
almost timeless design. A versatile collection with light,
minimalist lines, yet indisputably sturdy and durable.

The whole Cap Martin Sunset line (2019, Cappellini) includes extremely versatile sofas and coffee tables featuring clean, spare lines. Here Colombo finds inspiration in the elegantly vintage atmosphere of the fifties.

The elegance of the sartorial workmanship evident in the stitching is combined with a light and informal style as well as with the compositional modular composition in contrasting colors.

The collaboration between FontanaArte and Carlo Colombo gave rise to Milano 2015, the exclusive lamp dedicated to the city at Expo 2015 and forming a tie between the historic Milanese company and the designer.

The purely formal elegance of its lines, so geometric and pure, is achieved by having it produced in Carrara marble, the most precious kind, invariably favored by sculptors and artists for their creations. This lamp has an LED plate that sheds a magical light, enhancing the veining of the marble. Milano 2015 is a fabulously refined lamp, produced in a limited edition (only 100 pieces) worldwide.

2015

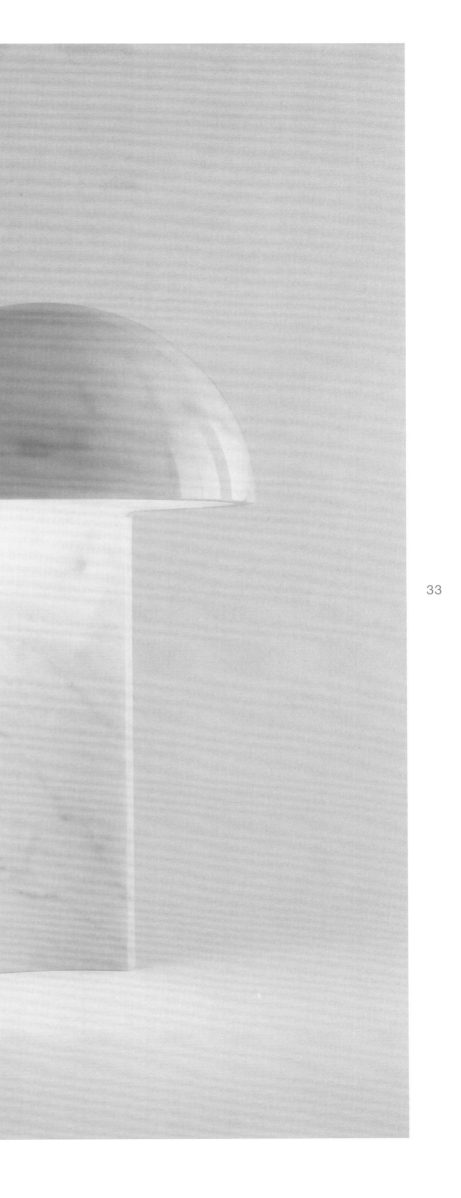

The Big Outdoor armchair is part of the Cloud outdoor collection (2010, Arflex). The frame, in powder-coated steel, usually concealed under the upholstery, is here left exposed, being clad only with the elastic rubber straps forming the seat and back.

SVEVA

The unmistakable Sveva armchair (2018, Flexform)
has a sinuous shell made from rigid polyurethane
covered in leather, with a soft seat and back cushions
padded with goose down. It has an aluminum base.

An armchair of indulgently contrasting forms: a rigid shell with delicate lines supports the comfortably padded upholstery.

A welcoming invitation
expressed by the ends of
the armrests, which spread
out with sinuous lines.

BUTTERFLY

The Butterfly sofa (2014, Bentley Home) masterfully interprets the Bentley Home philosophy. The soft cushions in leather or fabric enhance the deep seat, enclosed by the shell wholly finished in diamond quilting, defining an aesthetic with a concern for detail.

"The collections I designed for Bugatti Home, Bentley Home, and Trussardi Casa are part of a very ambitious lifestyle design project. The challenge stemmed from the desire to transfer the values of the Bentley and Bugatti brands, which have always been synonymous with luxury, innovation, and creativity, into the setting of the home. With the Trussardi brand, particular care is lavished on the fabrics and craftsmanship embodied in a taut and extremely sophisticated vocabulary, with an obsessive attention to detail."

ZIGO ZAGO

A minimalist concept, soft colors, and a modern mood in a carpet where the pattern is the playful synthesis of three overlapping rugs.

Made of wool and viscose fibers in orange, blue, and green, hand-tufted and made in India (2008, Cappellini).

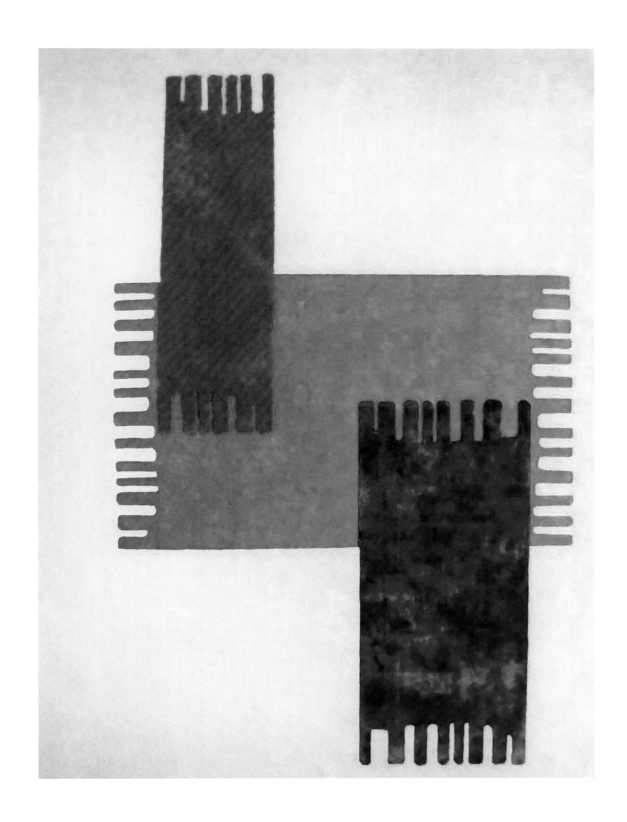

2008

Edmond (2013, Flexform) is a furniture series comprising armchair, sofa, and chaise longue. The simple yet refined sofa has a tubular steel frame covered with a macro-weave of padded fabric that creates its shape, contrasting with the generously padded seat and back cushions.

A sectional sofa having a markedly graphic design with the focus on the tubular steel frame. A generous aesthetic project to enhance the domestic landscape.

ALBUME

The poetry of contrasts: lightness and solidity, restraint and expressiveness, transparency and color.

Albume (2018, Antoniolupi) is another example of a freestanding washbasin designed by Carlo Colombo for Antoniolupi and the winner of the Wallpaper* Design Award 2019. Notable for its clean and minimalist forms, this washbasin comes in a wide range of variations and combinations of materials and refined color contrasts for the two pieces of base and bathtub. The layering of several geometric forms creates a perfect balance through the scrupulously studied proportions of its various parts. Albume comes to life in the contrast between the solid, durable base and the transparent colored basin that makes water the focus of interest.

48

Sinuous forms combine with clean and essential lines to renew the form of the washbasin.

Carlo Colombo strengthened his ties with the Antoniolupi brand by reinterpreting one of the most important bathroom accessories. Fluido (2022, Antoniolupi) is a new undermount washbasin. Drawing on the tradition of the washbasin set against the wall, Colombo presents his undermount version with large bowl and slender outlines that fits flush to the wall as a single sculptural piece.

2014

Eva grew out of the encounter between craft skills and technology, with elegant materials given special finishes capable of creating unique products.

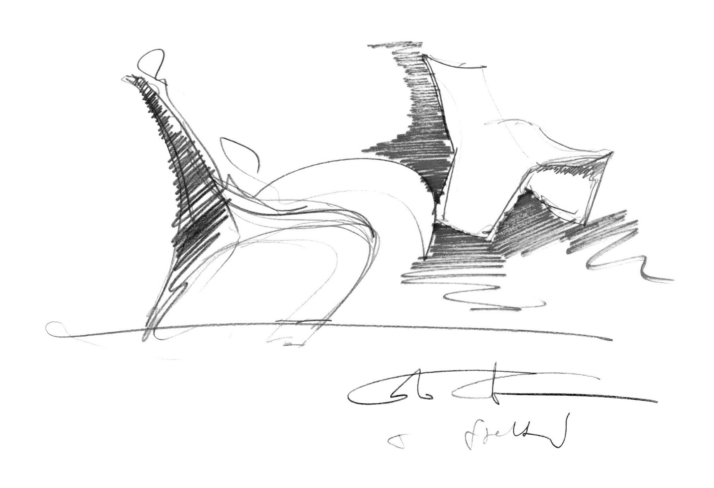

The name of the collection says everything. Eva (2014, Giorgetti) is the supreme tribute to women, with its sinuous and sensuous lines in the form of a bergère, pouf, and chair. Each of the elements has an external structure in painted plastic material with a metallic finish, created by a refined hand-crafted process. The collection is upholstered in fabric or leather.

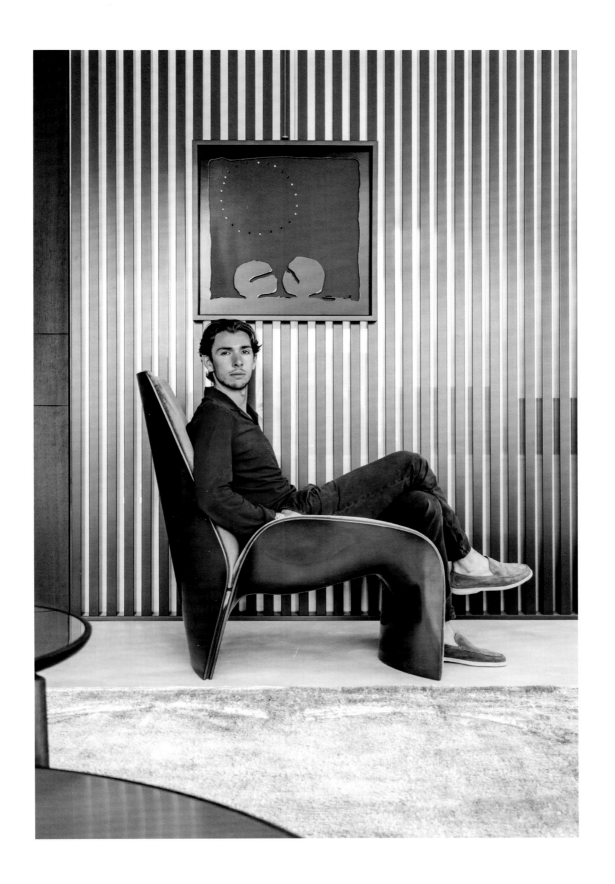

2017

Atlantic table and chairs (2017, Bugatti Home). A futuristic line that
also embodies close ties with the brand's history: the table top,
almost 10 feet (3 meters) long, is embellished with the form of the
legendary 1936 *Bugatti Atlantic*, from which it takes its name.

The slender carbon structure compresses profound innovations—based on art, form and material—into its fine lines.

Atlantic has a strongly linear, technological design, with pure, spare forms embellished with leather upholstery elegantly reinterpreting the theme of seating.

"It's as if the difference between the car and furniture has been effaced, with one becoming a natural continuation of the other."

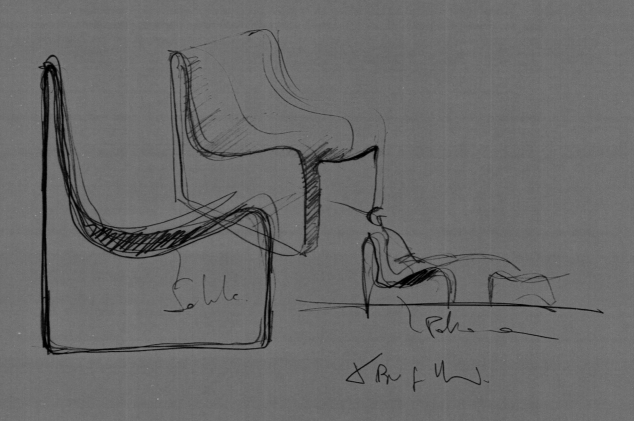

A chair with a slender technological structure in carbon
fiber (2017, Bugatti Home). The volumes are effaced
to create a piece that goes beyond minimalism,
approaching a degree of innovation based exclusively
on material and form. A pure, experimental design,
enriched by cognac-colored leather upholstery, which
reinterprets the idea of the chair with a new elegance.

AMALIA

MONACO

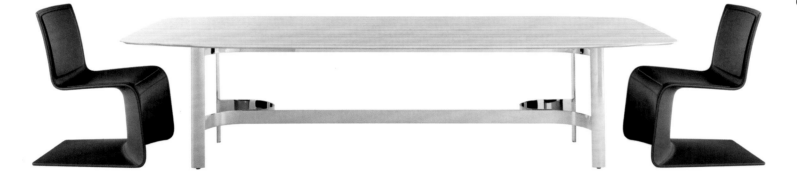

Clean and geometric lines in Monaco (2017, Bugatti Home), a table of the latest generation featuring a metal frame with gloss chrome finish. The top can be in lacquered wood, Steel Blue, or Titanium Silver, or in an alternative version in Olimpico striped marble.

The Royale sofa (2017, Bugatti Home) has generous volumes
and proportions that make it a presence with a great impact.
The outer shell is a single slightly flared element. Made of
carbon fiber, it shapes the soft leather armrests and back.
A veritable summons to comfort and relaxation.

ROYALE

A product of the creative and fruitful collaboration of the notable Antoniolupi brand and Carlo Colombo. Among the latest in bathtubs, Slope (2021) is a pure monolith that plays on the unexpected profile of the base rounded at the sides, which downplays its classicism. More than a simple bathroom element, it is a furniture sculpture.

69

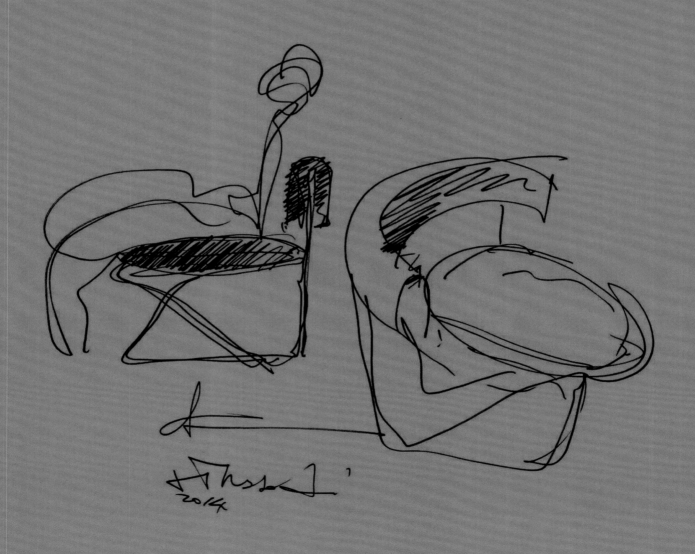

A-Round (2014, Trussardi Casa) is an iconic piece from the first Trussardi Casa collection. The armchair expresses the playful and diverting character of the Milanese brand, uniting "irony, coherence of handling, design, and fashion" and combining soft lines with elegant materials and finishes.

The Taylor set of cabinets (2018, Flexform) has sleek lines and geometric forms combined with refined details. The structure is in light burnished aluminum while the doors are faced with leather or an extensive range of wood veneers. The slender metal feet ensure the cabinets remain raised slightly, as if suspended off the floor. The cabinets can be arranged in multiple configurations, making Taylor furnishing accessories a flexible presence suited to the most varied home or office settings. Each is elegantly finished, including the back, enabling them to be placed in the center of a room.

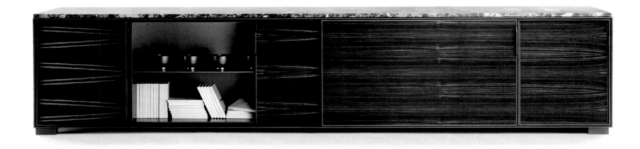

TAYLOR

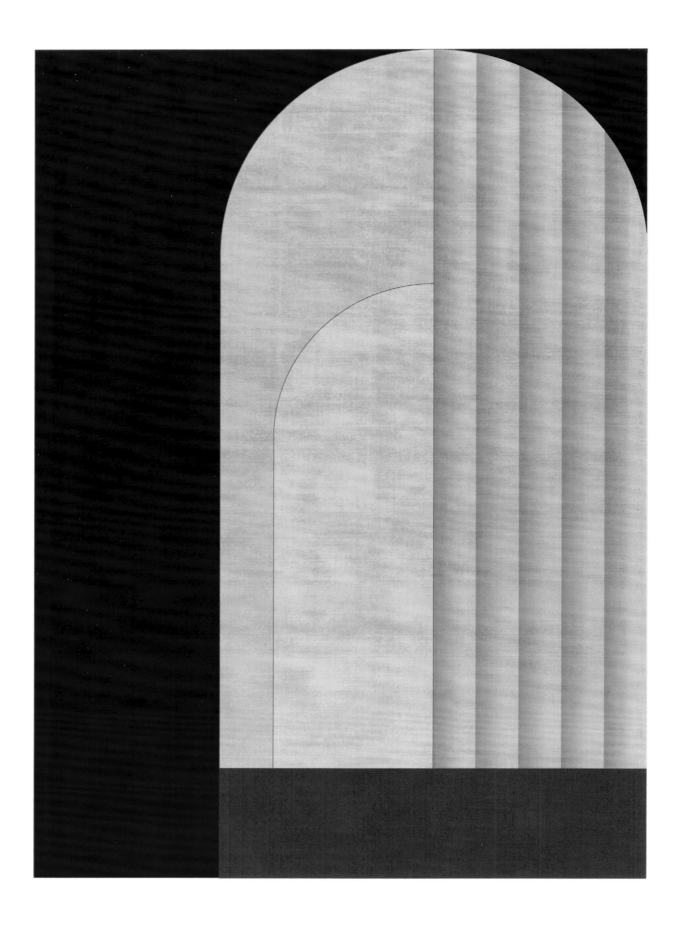

2022

The Sahrai collection of carpets (2022) forms an artistic composition. They are almost like paintings or tapestries with geometries and colors traceable to an abstract and contemporary interpretation of artistic expressions of the last century, between Metaphysical art and the Novecento movement.

2022

With overlapping and juxtaposed lines,
forms, and colors, Colombo creates abstract
landscapes that convey a concrete sense of
volume and depth, as if creating new backdrops
for one of the most refined domestic settings.

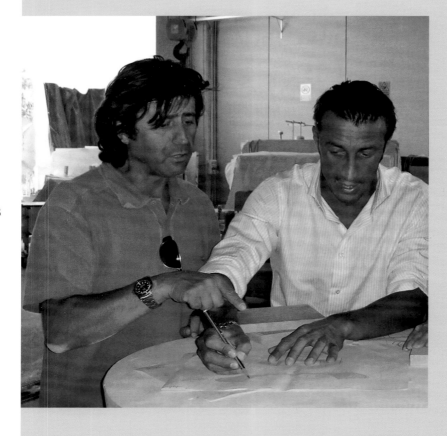

2008

A sculptural and sophisticated look for the Tuba freestanding washbasin (2008, Antoniolupi). Made of Flumood, it has a harmonic, archetypal, and sensuous form. A notable feature is that the exterior is available painted different colors.

The Baia bathtub (2013, Antoniolupi) can be made of
Cristalplant or stone. It is an object with pure yet organic
forms, modern yet with a classical imprint, a continuous
form in the absolute absence of sharp edges.

The bathtub achieves formal purity in the name of minimalism, functionality, and absolute classicism.

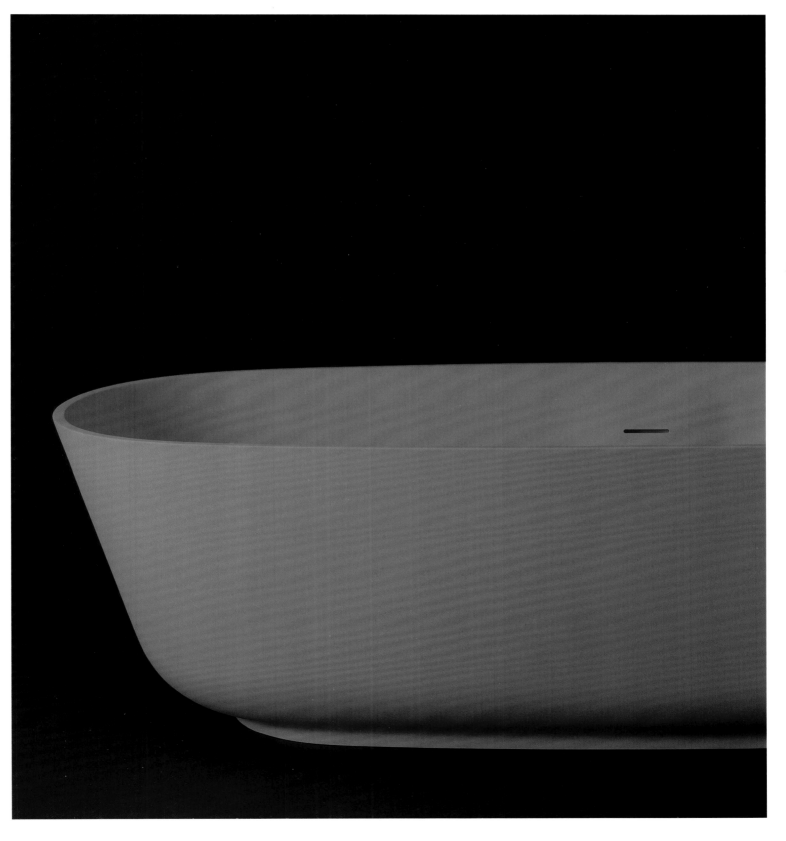

82

Leiston (2017, Bentley Home) is an elegant and sophisticated seating line that includes sofa, chaise longue, and armchair. It features an enveloping outer structure in precious briar covered with leather. The inside is again lined with leather, cool linen, and the finest cashmere velvet.

Special optional finishes are also available, such as diamond quilting on the inside of the structure closed with gunmetal steel toggles, or diamond quilting on the outside, and the logo embroidered on the backrest.

The Twelve kitchen (2009, Poliform) explores a new slim design with minimum thicknesses and maximum breadth of surfaces interacting with one another, the whole crowned with a broad range of possible finishes: from matt laminate to embossed or glossy lacquer, satin and polished glass with aluminum or black anodized support.

TWELVE

The Chloe bed (2017, Poliform), designed to be an oasis of comfort and a refuge from the stress of everyday life.

2017

Emblematic of an aesthetic of softness, the large padded headboard of this bed is designed to give an enveloping sense of welcome.

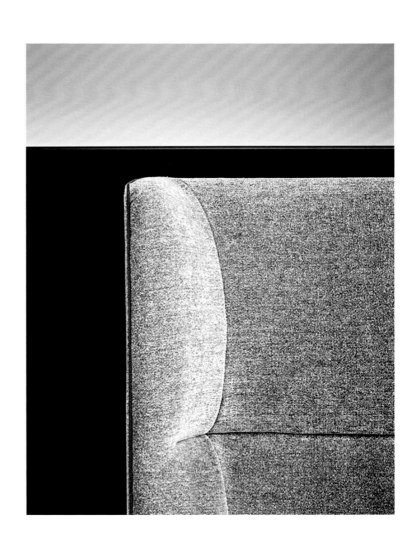

2020

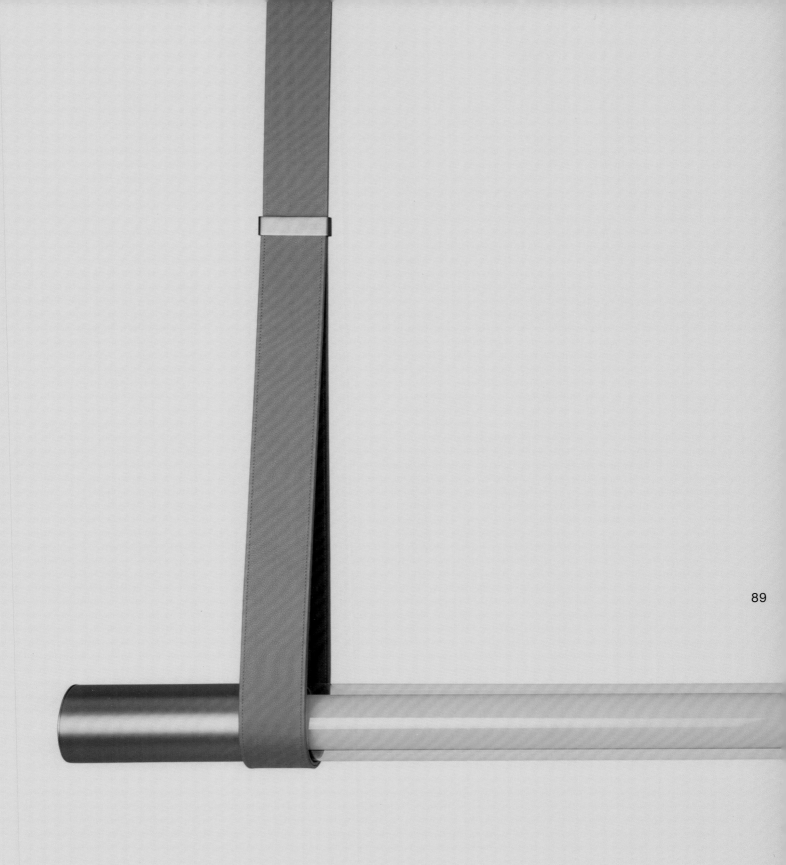

Sliver (2020, Giorgetti) is an LED suspension lamp that sheds a uniform, diffused light. The structure consists of a tubular diffuser in borosilicate glass with an opalescent finish, suspended by leather belts available in the following colors: powder, anthracite, or taupe. At the end of the glass bar the terminals are in metal with a pewter finish.

JE SUIS

A sculptural lamp made up of a two-tone sphere in white and silver glass and a monumental podium base in Carrara marble or wood. Je suis (2015, Penta Light) is a statement of intent, between the richness of the finishes and a beauty that goes beyond its function.

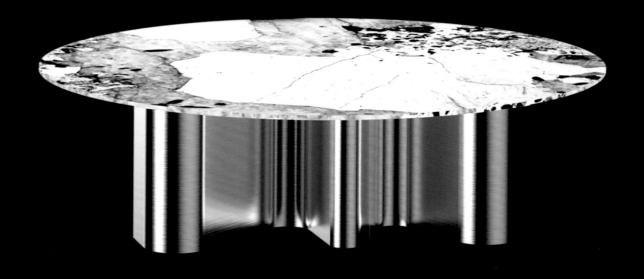

The Dunes tables (2020, Elie Saab Maison) bring
a refined and contemporary charm to any room.

Elite (2020, Elie Saab Maison) is a timeless classic, distinguished by its exclusive detailing and the exquisite craftsmanship of its futuristic lines. The frame is made of plywood and polyurethane foam. The fabric or leather upholstery of the collection can be enriched by a profile in leather or a brushed or bronzed satin gold finish; or even with blanket stitch seams. The base is made of brass.

With its ergonomic wraparound seat and the charm of its geometries, the Elite armchair (2020, Elie Saab Maison) adds a subtle touch of exclusiveness and elegance to convivial spaces as well as the workplace. The structure is in Polimex coupled with polyurethane foam, while the upholstery is in fabric or leather. This dining chair also comes in a two-tone version, with external leather upholstery and internal fabric or leather upholstery.

KNOKKE

The Knokke sofa and armchair (2014, Emmemobili) are one-piece furnishings CNC-shaped in solid plywood. Finished and sanded by hand, either with a natural finish or dyed in various colors. They come with a set of fitted cushions.

Scultura
il leg

Elegant swivel armchair Big Sveva (2022, Flexform), in a resin
structure covered in saddle leather/cowhide with a base in
polished steel, is worthy of the most sophisticated fifties offices.
It can also be produced as a single material piece, seamlessly
uniting seat and base in keeping with a more contemporary vision.

The Lugano handle was created from the desire to present a new model "made to measure" with a personality of its own.

For this line of handles, Colombo collaborated with Olivari (2018). The Lugano handle was part of the design of a house for an entrepreneur friend, for which he wanted to create a new model with a distinctive character. Colombo's expressive style is linear but also eclectic, evolving from a minimalist matrix to develop accents of unexpected compositional freedom with a logic closely bound up with the object's function.

Alberto Vignatelli and Carlo
Colombo sailing in Sardinia,
August 2016.

INDUSTRIAL DESIGN

Design is the focus of this book—design understood as a love of beautiful form, elegance, materials, and natural features inherent in Carlo Colombo's aesthetic and, at the same time, factors that have immediately enabled him to create a series of prolific partnerships with major players in the field of Italian design: Flexform, Poliform, Giorgetti, Cappellini, Antoniolupi, Artemide, Flou, Bentley Home, Bugatti Home, Trussardi Casa, Elie Saab Maison, Olivari, Faber, Penta Light, to name only a few. With them he shares a working method focused on the technical and structural processes and the definition of details, as well, naturally, as the choice of materials, including those with a high technological content. Over time, as Colombo himself relates, "The ties with these companies were consolidated and strengthened. The process of mutual growth became fertile and prolific." He traveled widely, his personal and professional growth continued and art, as mentioned, the designer's great interest and spiritual impulse, became an integral part of his projects. In this more mature phase, the cultural endowment that he had acquired over the years was expressed as an increasingly linear and austere design; but then he encountered the fascinating and experimental world of luxury. The language of design, its various strands and spheres, with endless opportunities to experiment with the formal, technical, and material potential of creativity, sometimes arose from special encounters with craftworkers, artists, cultural figures, and enlightened entrepreneurs. This is what happened with Alberto Vignatelli, a charismatic and visionary figure, empathetic, direct in his utterances and capable of

exporting Italian luxury from Forlì to the rest of the world with intelligent simplicity. As CEO and president of Luxury Living Group, he introduced Carlo Colombo to the magnificent and "unlimited" universe of luxury, initiating an important path of research and expressiveness, creativity and a passion for materials that has become the hallmark of the designer and his output of luxury items in the last decade. His love of cars is also in synergy with his professional career in this respect. Following his encounter with Bentley and Bugatti cars, he created a line of furnishings and accessories, as well as working with well-known fashion brands, first Fendi and then, above all, Trussardi, an opportunity that enabled Colombo to change the paradigm of his own way of thinking, which underwent a further evolution. This collaboration gave rise to the ironic and sophisticated A-Round in gilded metal and refined fabrics. In more recent years he has been working with the fashion designer Elie Saab, as in the other cases designing a line of home furnishings in harmony with the fashion house's creative hallmark. Here the elegance of an almost courtly thirties restraint is expressed in the Kate armchair, with its allusions to the interiors of Frank Capra's movies and the fashions of the period. It appears again in the iconic Majesty sofa, of course, but with an unexpected metallic structure left modernly visible at the base and then repeated in the profile of the large armrests at the sides. This strand in his work extends all the way to the more enveloping Elite series with a cocoon design evoking the Italian thirties age of white telephones in the absence of corners replaced by wonderful curved shapes.

ASIA

Spirituality in the service of technology and the most extreme styling.

Carlo Colombo's travels in Asia form a very important chapter of his research, devoted to the continuous development of his vocabulary and his working method. "It's a completely different culture from ours," says the designer. "Asia is a sentimental journey of the self, it calls out a constant confrontation with the soul. A journey toward oneself. Asian culture is deeply respectful of body and soul, of reflection and respite." Colombo has visited Asia at least a hundred times. His first trip was to Japan, followed by Thailand, Malaysia, Singapore, and China. With the Japanese world in particular he felt a mutual fascination which, in 2004 in Tokyo, saw him receive his first international award as Designer of the Year. During this period he created the iconic Sushi armchair for Zanotta (2005), followed a year later by Bali (2006, Poliform), an homage to Achille Castiglioni's complex simplicity. Then there ensued his unbroken relationship with China, including his work as a designer of

architecture, to which has been added his teaching post at the University of Beijing (2011). "The Asian experience is always intense," Colombo observes, so much so that he can trace unexpected influences in the approach and attention to detail and materials and the exclusiveness of his luxury designs for Bentley. Examples are the Tiverton chaise longue (2020), the elegant Dunes coffee tables (2020) in metal and precious marble designed for Elie Saab Maison, and the magnificent leather cabinets that recall the most sophisticated Chinese and Japanese display cases. Finally, the Middle East appears in his choice of gilded metals, in the play of light and shade, in the metallic geometries worthy of the finest mashrabiyas in the steel bases of tables as well as in the dark marbles and the comfort of sofa such as the Elite for Elie Saab Maison (2020) or the series of soft and imposing Jaipur (2020) and Amal beds for Flou (2019).

ART
カラオケ歌広場
センター街
カラオケ
歌広場
NEW ALBUM
5.23
RELEASE
渋谷センター街
消火栓
渋谷
おとなり
サンデー
Panasonic
McDonald's
&
パーティー
1F/2F
105席
センタービル
BURGER KING
B1F
SUSHI

The Jaipur bed (2020, Flou) features modern boiserie with framed macro weaves of wood with a slender metal profile, almost a fabric with weft and warp dilated endlessly, as in an original reinterpretation of the sartorial skill of Flou's textile tradition.

Charlotte (2018, Giorgetti) is a project that looks at the tradition of postwar Italian design with a contemporary taste and an elegance afforded by luxury materials and finishes.

Each component of this collection expresses a refined study of the details: the metal feet are a structural and expressive feature. The top is a choice between wood and marble, in each case presenting a new interpretation of the design. Inside, the system of shelves and compartments can be personalized and varied to ensure almost endless functionality.

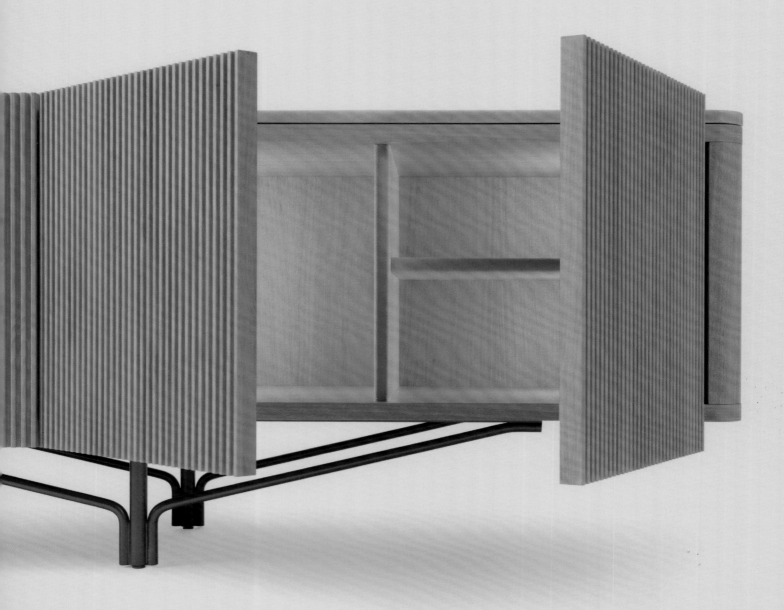

2018

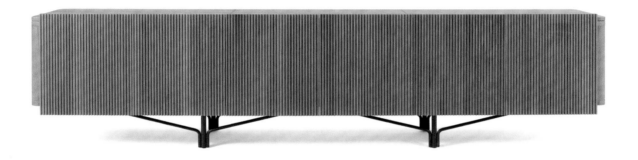

AMAL

The Amal bed (2019, Flou) is embellished
with elegant metal trim at the sides of
the headboard that clasp the covering
and enhance the softness of the whole.

The Sushi armchair (2005, Zanotta) reveals an evident
Eastern inspiration. Here Colombo opts for a full
and comfortable seat, in matching fabric or leather,
combined with the wooden frame that echoes
Japanese chopsticks and, in a subtle contrast, plays
with the slightly curved lines of the wooden armrests.

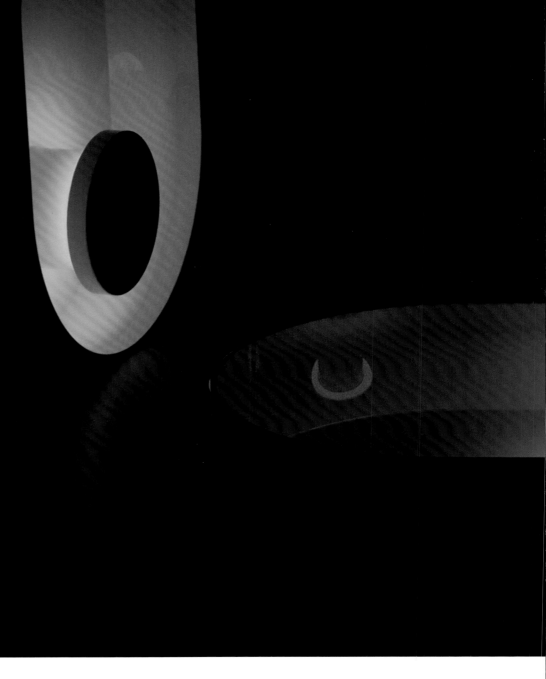

2022

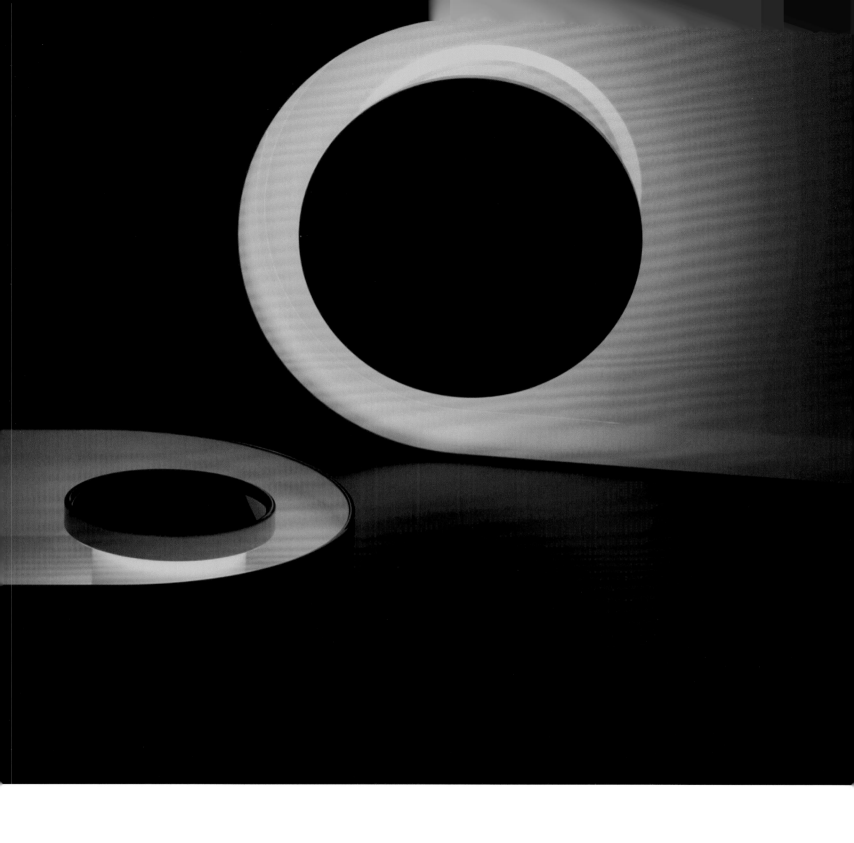

Eclipse (2022, Antoniolupi). A collection of luminous washbasins with an elliptical form and circular internal support island and highlighted by a perimeter of recessed LED lighting in different colors.

BARREL

Its rounded forms taken from the archetype of the wooden barrel, together with its massive, striking, and iconic form make Barrel a design object outside time and place.

Barrel (2003, Antoniolupi) is one of the iconic products from Antoniolupi, a best seller since it was first presented. A pure, solid, and compact monolith softened by its slightly curving profile with a perfectly smooth surface that immediately occupies the space as the dominant feature of the composition. As simple in form as it is complex in craftsmanship, it is a true sculpture available in stone, marble, or onyx, as well as a more modern version in Cristalplant.

The careful choice of materials, combining the rigid yet softened structure in the lattice design with the abundant padded seat covered in fabric, gives a sense of comfort and freshness to this outdoor furniture.

124

Outdoor Aldìa (2021, Giorgetti) is the latest addition to the well-known brand's outdoor collection. It has a distinctive structure in die-cast and extruded aluminum supporting the upholstered fabric seat, and sides and backs with geometries evoking the composition of an architectural facade in wood layered and pantographed with a plastic CNC machine.

The care lavished on the detailing is defined in every combination of forms and materials. An intriguing detail is the sinuous leather armrest "buttoned" to the frame supporting the padded seat and back.

Giorgetti enriches its outdoor collection with a set of small tables with metal frames and with tops in Palladiana, a composition of marble and granite. In this way Colombo enhances its outdoor furnishings with quality materials and elegance of a kind usually found only in interiors.

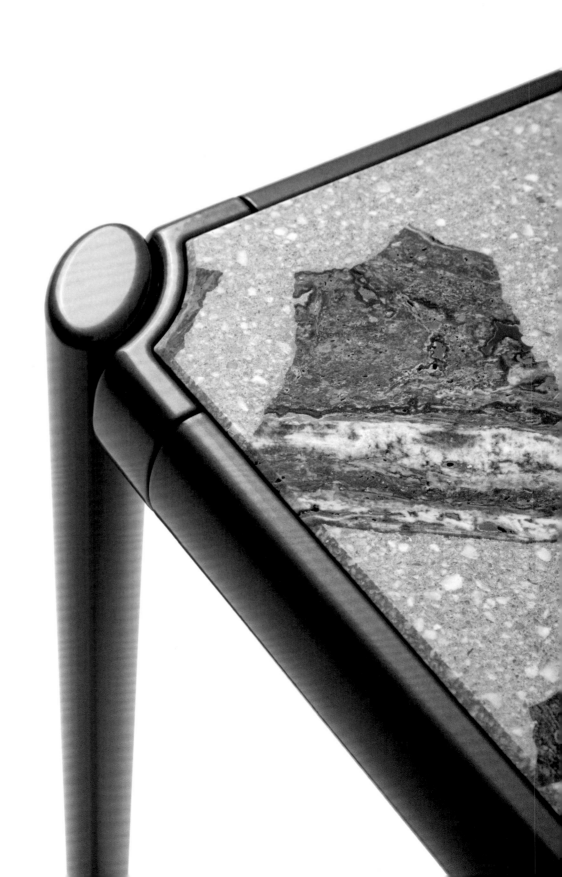

SHIRLEY

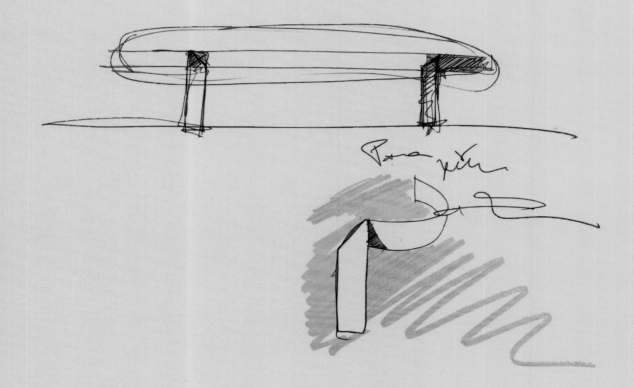

The Shirley padded bench (2021, Giorgetti) is a soft oval
furnishing enclosed and supported by a ribbon-shaped frame.

A double bed with clean, taut lines (2019, Flou), it immediately evokes an impression of discreet, unostentatious luxury. The rigorous form of the headboard, framed by the precious metal structure that descends to form the feet, is softened and made to appear slimmer by the fabric expertly stitched with vertical quilting, giving the bed a welcoming and sophisticated design.

KOI

The Oval chair (2021, Trussardi Casa) is one of the latest creations to enter the luxury living portfolio. Heralded by the name, the central feature of the design is the metal oval tracing the outline of a medieval coat of arms, at once expressing the iconic Italian spirit of the Milanese brand. Refined in materials and finishes, the chair features details in dark chocolate Vermont leather with Trussardi's Greyhound logo print.

ELIE SAAB

MAISON

L'Infini (2022, Elie Saab Maison) is definitely an icon of the
well-known fashion and design brand, with a direct and
symbolic allusion to the concept of "infinity," an emblem
of favorable augury in various cultures around the world.

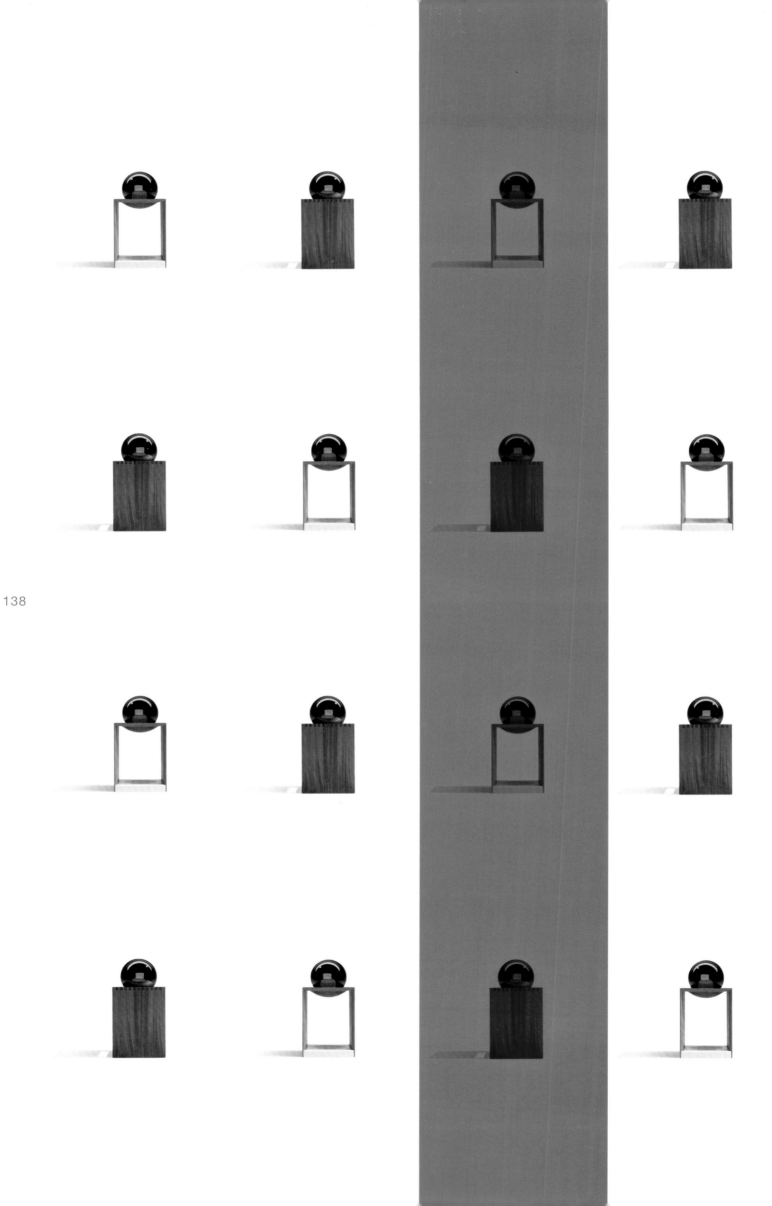

138

A table lamp
with a double
sphere in
reflective glass
of variable
colors resting
delicately on
a solid wood
structure.

Spaziotempo (2020, Giorgetti)
is embellished by the elegant detail
of the comb joint between the sphere
and the Calacatta marble base.

The clean, uncluttered lines are combined with refined forms and materials. The eye-catching feature is the extraordinary expressiveness of leather as a noble and versatile material embodied in the continuity of the upholstery, which even covers the legs.

This masterly design of the Isabel line (2013, Flexform) makes it perfect for matching harmoniously with any setting. The leather upholstery covers the metal frame, while on the formal level the ergonomic back extends toward the armrests, spreading out at the extremities and so creating a delicate fold evoking the Japanese art of origami.

ISABEL

COBRA CHAIR

A contemporary reinterpretation of the first version of the Cobra chair designed in 1902 by Carlo Bugatti, this innovative, avant-garde piece expresses a new stylistic impulse while respecting its original vocabulary. The base, seat, and back unfold along a single form with curved and sinuous lines upholstered in leather, interrupted only at the point where the coattails would have fitted.

Cobra Chair (2017, Bugatti Home) is made of carbon and padded with leather upholstery. This is an iconic piece in the collection of furnishings.

The sensuous, tapering shell flows into the armrests, shaped like wings opening outward.

RAMSEY

The Ramsey line (2021, Bentley Home) consists of
sofa, loveseat, and armchair. The lines are delicate,
interrupted only by a fascinating transparency between
seat and back. The gunmetal insert frames the profile of
the structure up to the seat, underscoring its seeming
suspension. The structure can be covered in veneer,
briar wood, or fully upholstered in leather or fabric.

AGO

Ago (2020, Giorgetti), an oval coffee table
in solid black walnut that takes its name from
the slender legs (*ago* in Italian means "needle").

A light, minimalist line creates this refined design with a skillful combination of materials: solid wood for the legs and marble or plywood veneered and bordered with solid wood for the top. It combines the linearity of Scandinavian design with Italian postwar elegance in a design beyond time and place.

Town (2014, Giorgetti) is a chest of drawers that can be composed as wished, vertically or horizontally, meeting the desire for an ever more personalized contemporary living space to fulfill our individual needs.

The home interior is renewed with this fully modular storage unit.

BALI

Bali (2006, Poliform) is an attractive and amusing armchair with chromed metal base and a structure in molded polyurethane padded with polyester upholstery. The broad seat, conceived as a single piece supported by a light metal structure, becomes a comfortable and private gesture of lighthearted modernity.

The Altea bed (2016, Giorgetti) is a tribute to
functionality in the essence of the design combined
with the richly luxurious sense of its presence. The
contemporary design is distinguished by the sinuous
and enveloping curve of the headboard that invites you
to relax and designs the wall against which it is set.

2016

The slender line of the backrest and the arched form of the base define the uniquely distinctive style of the Berenice chair (2016, Fendi Casa), designed to furnish every setting with a harmonious and almost sculptural presence.

2017

Winner of the Wallpaper* Design Award 2017 in the "Best Landing Pad" category, Drive (2017, Giorgetti) displays a simple yet refined design made up of details and materials that make it special, reserved, and innovative: very Milanese.

DRIVE

SWING

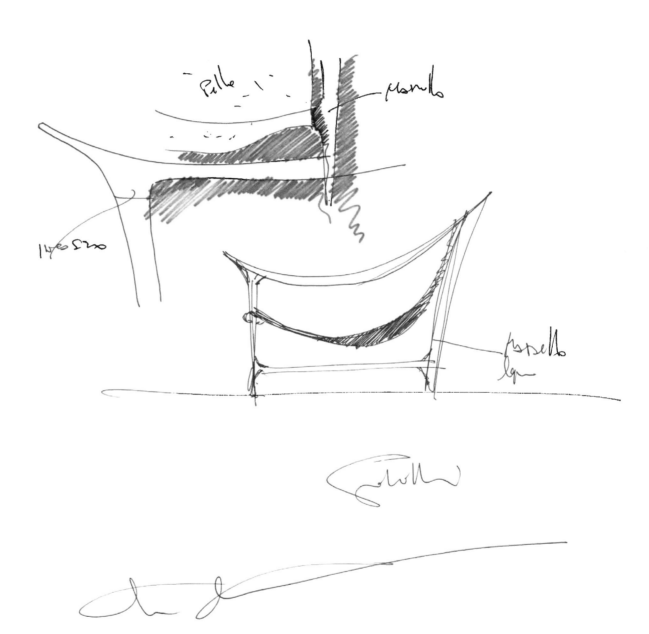

The Swing sculpture-armchair (2015, Giorgetti) has a unique design and refined style, with forms spanning the past and modernity. The structure is in solid black walnut, with the curved seat in polyurethane foam upholstered in leather.

NORTH AMERICA

American pragmatism becomes rational elegance.

Colombo's relationship with the United States is dichotomous, not a "spiritual," enveloping relationship, as in the case of Asia in its various facets and expressions. Here the fascination lies in the elegance of luxurious New York interiors, with the frame of reference provided by design icons from the forties and fifties such as Knoll, Mies, Breuer, and Saarinen, and expressed with award-winning pieces such as the Drive sofa for Giorgetti, winner of the Wallpaper* Design Award 2017, or the Atlantic series with their unique geometries upholstered in leather or the Monaco table with its "less is more" lines, both for Bugatti Home. America also means the absolute comfort of the infinite Newbridge sofa for Flexform, and again of the Isabel chairs (also for Flexform, 2013) and the Chloe bed for Poliform (2017), which could have been designed for an interior of a movie set. Here the verticality of the skyscrapers, the penthouses, the offices of the big brands that Colombo works for make for a continuous reversal of points of view, forms, and proportions. He responds to New York as an immensely stimulating city, with a unique energy revealing new visions through his creative gifts.

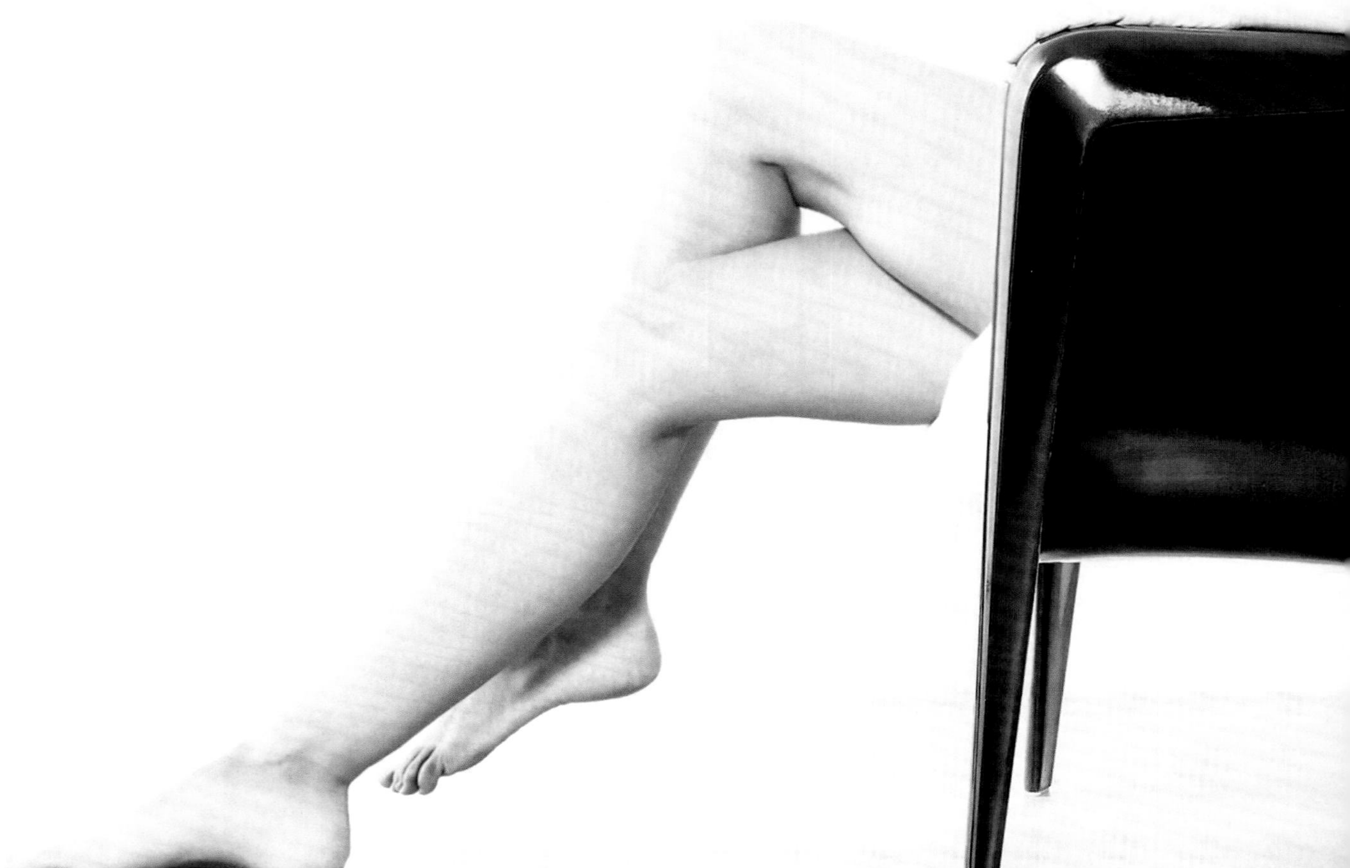

The pairing of a sturdy shell in rigid polyurethane with a soft goose down cushion. This is the impression made by Cocca (2006, Arflex), as the perfect synthesis of hardness and softness. Polyurethane is a symbol of modernity and durability, while goose down ensures the seat offers a sense of comfort and welcome.

A welcoming sensation combined with the appearance of formal grace are the effect of harmonious proportions, sinuous lines, and generous padding that offer the utmost in comfort and conviviality.

The Newbridge seating system (2018, Flexform) has an enveloping cocoon effect heightened by the special reclinable armrest that can be set at different angles. On the outside it features elegant piping and an elegant metal bar near the upholstery fold. The base, seats, backrests, and armrests have extra soft padding in a special elastic material that is non-deformable yet flexible and extraordinarily soft, making it breathable, durable, and, above all, comfortable. The refined die-cast metal feet ensure the sofa remains slightly suspended off the floor. Newbridge is a highly modular seating system that can be personalized to create compositions of variable dimensions that adapt to every type of space.

2019 GOLD WINNER
EUROPEAN PRODUCT DESIGN AWARD
www.productdesignaward.eu

The enduring partnership between Carlo Colombo and Flexform is embodied in a number of iconic pieces designed for the well-known Italian brand. In 2018 they were the Sveva armchair, the Newbridge sofa, the Taylor cabinet, and the Gustav series of tables.

BERRY

Extending the Flexform outdoor range
is the Berry (2021) series of coffee and
dining tables with tops in molded ceramic
or wood and a slender, elegant steel
structure painted dark gray. The lightness
is expressed by a base with a minimalist
design, consisting of a pattern of slender
metal spokes contrasting with the thick
wooden top veneered in American black
walnut or ash, available in multiple colors.

A charming contemporary furnishing,
simple yet also suitable for interiors.

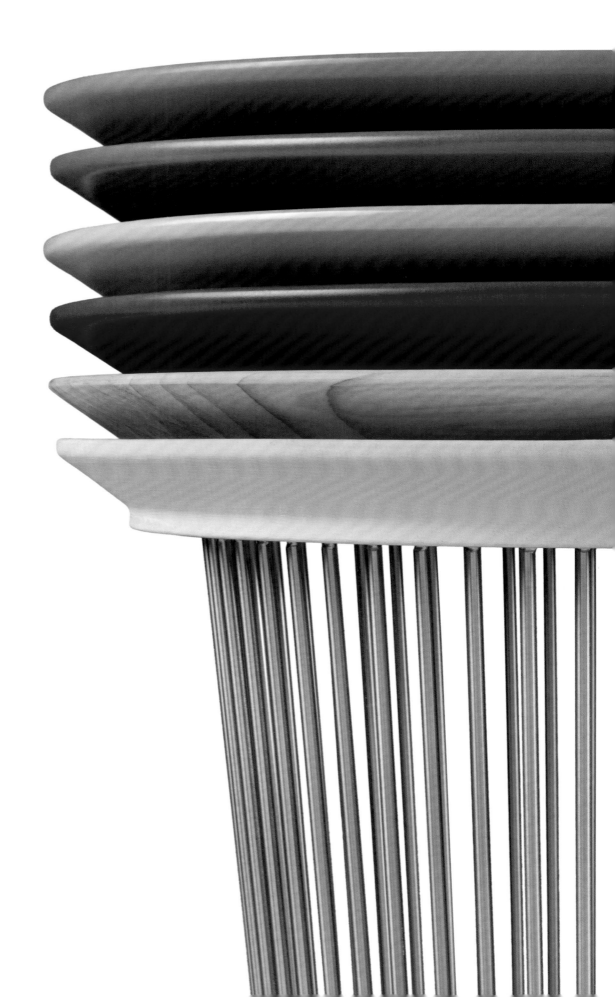

HESTER

An armchair with elegant lines and compact proportions well suited to any setting, whether paired with vintage or hyper contemporary pieces. In its apparent simplicity, Hester (2014, Trussardi Casa) presents a wealth of almost sartorially elegant details. The soft wooden structure supports the seat and back, whose curvature recalls fifties ergonomics and the outlines of the petals of a flower.

PARK 1

Park 1 (2018, Poliform) is a light and elegant
contemporary bed with minimalist forms and
die-cast steel feet.

ALISON

Lightweight and stylish, the Alison Outdoor armchair (2018, Flexform) is the outdoor version of the same indoor chair, preserving the quality of its design and interpreting it in materials that ensure its durability in the open air.

The sinuous lines of the structure of the armchair are in painted extruded aluminum, while the base is made of marine plywood. The back is in polyurethane foam upholstered with a removable fabric.

OUTDOOR

Compact proportions for a timeless style that goes beyond fashions. The tradition of Scandinavian design is reinterpreted in a modern way for an experience of absolute comfort.

The sinuous lines of the structure support the generously padded seat, while the leather backrest offers particularly comfortable support. Innumerable color-material combinations can be obtained by pairing the aluminum structure, also available in solid black walnut or ash wood stained in a wide range of shades as varied as they are original, with the leather backrest available in nine colors. The padded seat can be upholstered in the complete range of fabrics and leathers from the exclusive Flexform collection. Thanks to its compact proportions and timeless charm, the Alison Outdoor armchair is perfectly at home in every setting.

HAPP

Happ is a new system of modular sofas (2017, Trussardi Casa) with slender geometries that would have appealed to Vico Magistretti, interpreted in contemporary styles. The rational lines are softened by the smoothed and rounded edges of the back and arms, with the profile picked out in contrasting piping. Presented in light gray fabric upholstery, embellished by the cushions with a lightly quilted allover logo motif, it is flanked by an ottoman added as a separate element with forms reflecting the geometry of the sofa.

Young and contemporary design, a project for everyday life, an open invitation to comfort and conviviality.

184

Sit 414 (2015, Trussardi Casa) has a steel frame
with gunmetal finish, which takes the form of a
profile with clear lines and accentuated angles
cradling the comfortable leather seat. Together with
the coordinated anchor straps, they make the seat
an object of style and elegance with finely curated
details. The design of the armchair expresses a new
compositional direction in which each structural
element has its own precise aesthetic value.

TRAIL

The Trail kitchen (2015, Poliform) is a contemporary conception of the kitchen. Its distinguishing feature is the recessed Trail handle, which can be positioned at the center or the ends of the doors. The search for minimum thicknesses is the unifying detail of the different components of the model, from the tops to the shelves for the boiserie and the open units lit from the back.

The feature
distinguishing Trail
from other kitchens
is the recessed handle
system and the
minimum thickness
of its components.

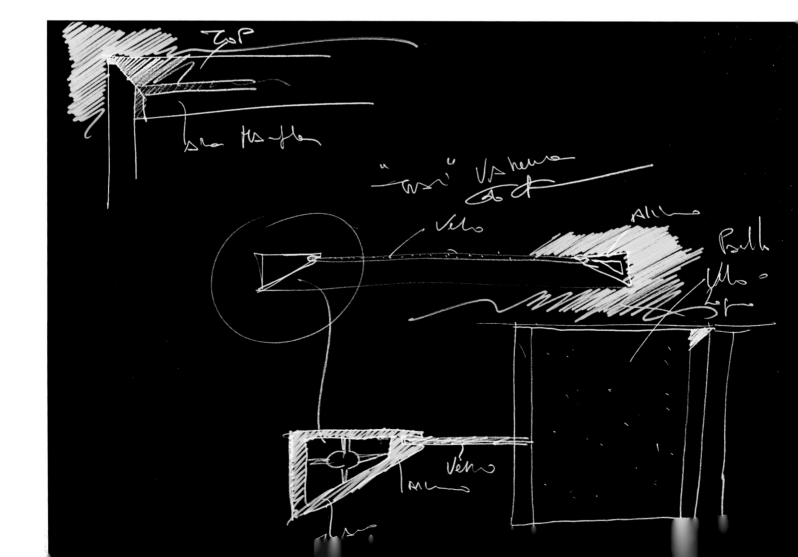

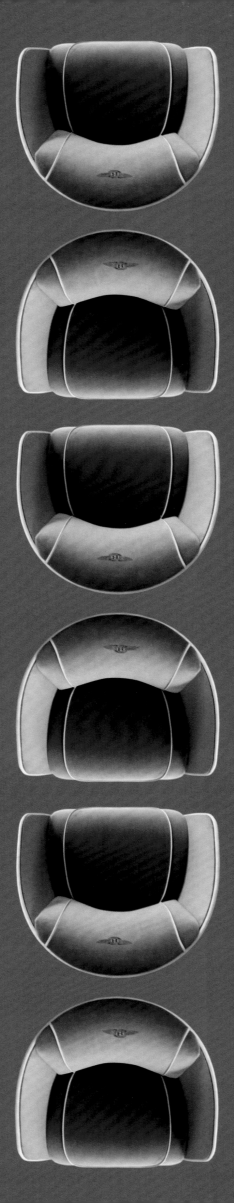

RUGBY

The finely proportioned outlines
of the Rugby lounge chair
(2014, Bentley Home) recall the
atmosphere of a 1940s golf club.

The elegance of the collection enhances the manufacturer's craftmanship with contemporary lines, precious materials, and refined proportions.

The Urban collection of sofas and armchairs (2015, Giorgetti) is inspired by metropolitan and industrial design. It transcends time with references to the sophisticated creations of the masters of the fifties in a completely contemporary vision of wood and technological materials.

SOFTWING

Softwing (2016, Flou) is a collection interpreted in a range
of furnishings, including bed, armchairs, pouf, and lamp to
complete the sleeping quarters. Here the armchair, with the
backrest offered in two heights, has a sinuous form with a
markedly decorative effect. The curved outer shell, made of
precious wood—walnut, ebony or larch—supports a soft and
comfortable interior upholstered in removable fabric or leather.

Carlo Colombo developed the concept of a contemporary island kitchen as the focus of life inside the home, a coherent entwining of paths with a single shared point.

Carlo Colombo designed ISØLA (2020, Rossana) by reinterpreting a historic kitchen produced by Rossana, making it the utmost evolution of the kitchen as the center of the domestic space. It was a project developed as a high-end product with transversal uses and functions. A model expressed in the form of a monobloc with architectural geometries, close to the idea of furniture thanks to the materials chosen. An open kitchen ready to engage in a dialogue with the surrounding space, revealed through clearly defined forms and strongly marked features, designed to fit into any environment. A journey through five places where the project takes shape and recounts Rossana's style through beauty and its material contents.

195

ISØLA

198

Thorne (2018, Bentley Home) is an elegant armchair embodying compactness and comfort without sacrificing style. The Bentley logo is printed on the back. The detailing of the seams and the combination between upholstery and structure are notable for their refinement.

Brightness, transparency, lightness: a glass sphere that enhances the glow of light with an interplay of reflections between the lamp itself and its setting.

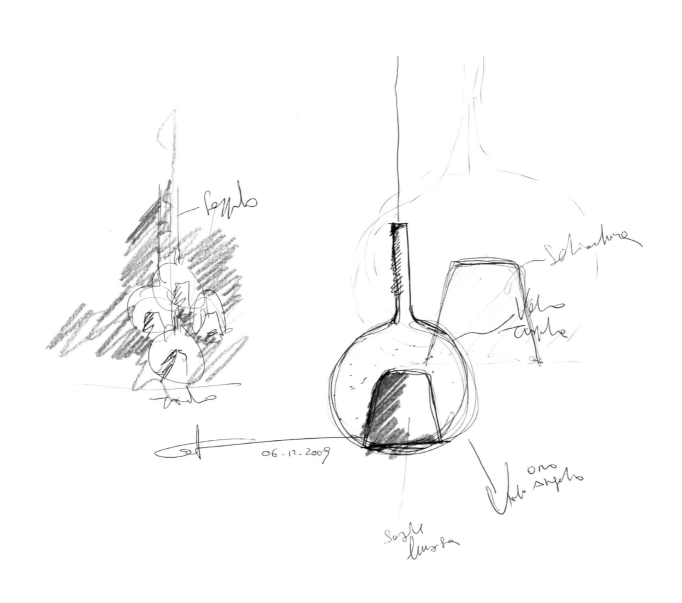

2019 PLATINUM WINNER
EUROPEAN
PRODUCT
DESIGN
AWARD
www.productdesignaward.eu

203

Glo (2009, Penta Light) is an iconic set of lamps that come in table, floor, and suspension versions. The series offers numerous possible compositions by size and color. The lamps were included in the *Quirinale Contemporaneo* 2021 exhibition at the Palazzo del Quirinale, the residence of the president of Italy.

RAMSEY

The Ramsey Bed also belongs to the well-known collection previously devised by Carlo Colombo for Bentley Home (2020), with a series of sofas whose detailing it replicates. This comfortable, innovative bed has hinged wings on either side, here with white leather inner lining and functional pockets, borrowed from automobile fittings and reflecting the distinctive style of the well-known British carmaker. In this case the structure is in smoked liquid amber, but other versions and materials are also available.

The Ettore Grand Bureau Desk (2017, Bugatti Home)
is designed for thinking big and rests on the idea that
a style typical of Italy in the twentieth century should
not be forgotten. The elongated plane of the worktop
slopes gently until it develops seamlessly into the
base of the desk, with its innovative design made
possible by using carbon for the structure.

206

From cars to home and office furnishings, Bugatti has transferred the codes of its historic brand into a luxurious, contemporary, elegant, and exclusive line of furnishings.

A clearly marked, decisive profile
is the hallmark of this collection designed
by Carlo Colombo for Antoniolupi (2021).
Purity of form and compositional flexibility
accompany the powerful graphic design
of the frame, which is used to affirm a style
and design a domestic landscape made
up of voids and solids, refined chromatic
color pairings, reflections, and an interplay
of light and shade.

Bigger coffee tables (2012, Poliform) with solid
wooden structure and fiber or marble tops.

Curved tops and rounded corners define this collection of coffee tables. They pay tribute to the most sophisticated tradition of last century's design with a contemporary, informal touch.

The Diana chair (2013, Giorgetti) is an elegant element for the living room. The outside is covered with leather and fabric upholsters the inside.

DIANA

Perfect details,
total comfort,
impeccable design,
and quality materials
in this pragmatic
and timeless seat for
indoors and outdoors.

214

A strong and decisive design for Icon
(2018, Flou), a double bed with an
essential, almost minimalist character
softened by the striking textile component.
The softly padded headboard contrasts
pleasantly with the refined metal trim.

A symbol of elegance and refinement. The
Hermann armchair (2019, Fendi Casa) is designed
to create an atmosphere poised between past
and present. Its lines are rational and geometric
yet also fluid, with the curved forms cradling the
padded seat and enveloping the sitter the way the
historic bergère once did. It deliberately contrasts
the padded leather upholstery of the shell with the
wooden structure of the base.

Jeremy (2019, Flexform) reveals and conceals, a dichotomy that inspired the concept embodied in this family of sideboards. Their pure lines and sleek volumes form a harmonious alternation of voids and solids for displaying and containing in compartments with drop-front doors.

SOUTH AMERICA

The fascination of modernity in dialogue with nature.

This is Brazil, with its rich contrasts between luxury and simplicity, tradition and modernism.
It is the home of eclecticism, with the designer's gaze embodied in the stylistic variety of his pieces inspired by places, local craftsmanship, the intense presence of nature and materials, as well as high-tech experiments. As a designer, Colombo encounters, explores, and understands South America, delivering lectures like the one he gave in São Paulo. The continent's influence appears in colorful works like the Opale washbasin for Antoniolupi (2018), as well as the simplicity of Lina Bo Bardi in the magnificent Big Outdoor armchair for Arflex (2010), or the Twelve kitchen for Poliform

(2009), which seems to arise from the sophisticated tropical-brutalist linearism of the villas designed by the Pritzker Prize–winning architect Paulo Mendes da Rocha. Furnishings are also the ideal response to a given program, the synergy between creativity and rationality of approach and process, the encounter between a European designer and his client, whether he is working for a highly recognizable brand whose mood he amplifies or emphasizes, or a well-known manufacturer whose character is clearly defined, and from which he can only set off in an independent but not opposing direction. In all these ways, South America is another place for experimentation and inspiration.

An informal but sophisticated style distinguishes this sectional outdoor sofa.

The Eddy sofa (2019, Flexform) for
outdoors features a metal structure
upholstered with elegant polypropylene
fiber woven entirely by hand.

LARZIA

Larzia (2015, Trussardi Casa) is synonymous with comfort and softness, with its full form enclosing a volume that is generous yet open and light. The Larzia armchair is defined by the fascia binding seat and back together, giving it stability and enhancing its refined contemporary style. The structure is in steel and wood while the seat can be upholstered in leather or fabric with contrasting stitching combined with the fascias of the armrests.

The contrast of materials, forms, and colors, between gloss metals and Carrara marble, embellish the formal sleekness of the volumes.

An astronomical interplay of hemispheres inspires the Elisabeth collection (2017, Penta Light)—from the more composed table version to the Art Deco overtones of the suspension lamp and wall system.

BENTLEY

OUTDOOR

The collaboration with the well-known Bentley Home
brand continues with Carlo Colombo designing
a new outdoor line, in which an eye-catching feature
is the original interlacing back that lightens its impact,
making it perfectly attuned to an outdoor setting.

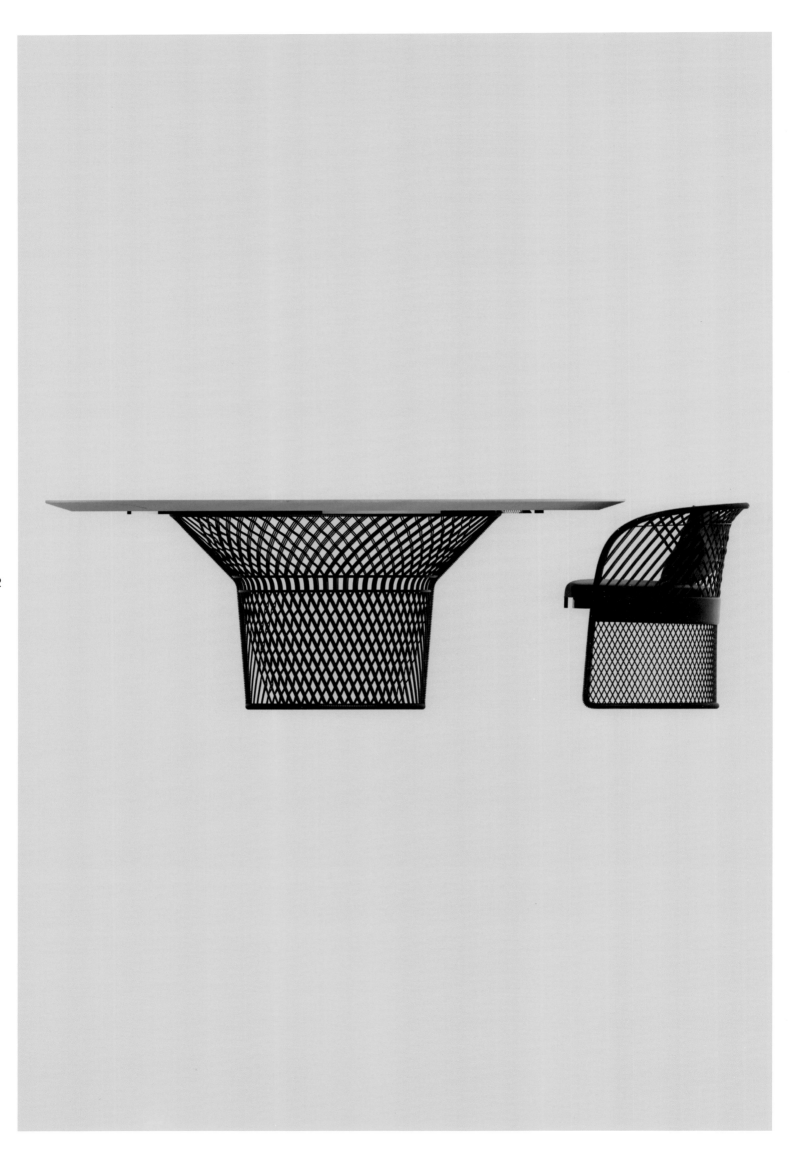

Also part of the Bentley Home line,
a series of seats and tables repeat
the style of the sofa inspired by nature.
Interlacing metal profiles become an
enlarged macro decoration respectively
for backrest and base, completing
the ideal set of outdoor furnishings.

Mere (2019, Bentley Home) is
the perfect lounge seat. With its
compact volume and cockpit layout,
it has a refined larch structure that
harmoniously embraces the backrest
and seat in leather or fabric, the effect
of the whole heightened by a slender
metal profile encircling the base.

GENTLEMAN

Gentleman (2014, Flou) is a bed with an impressive line
with the headboard available in two heights, high or low.
The distinctive double covers are like "a dress that slips off
the headboard" giving it a character of distinctive elegance.
A second removable padded cover for the headboard
features a cord trim along the corners of the base and
the perimeter, tone-on-tone or in a contrasting shade.

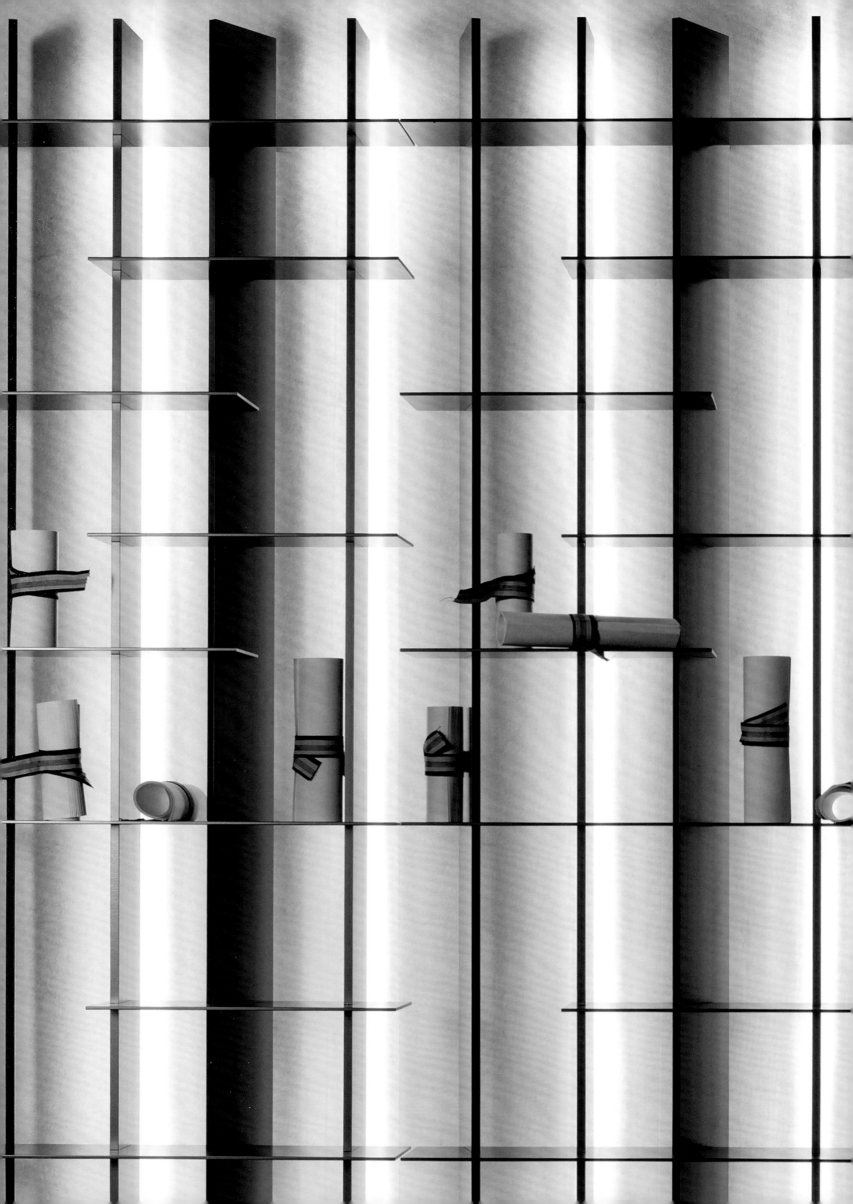

239

The CCLight bookcase (2013, Natevo)
is a modular luminous wall system
designed by Colombo for Natevo.
It gives light a starring role, imparting
lightness, atmosphere, and a touch
of magic to its setting. A lamp-
bookcase in 20-inch (30-centimeter)
modules, it has offset shelves and
a slender, elegant structure in
aluminum profile. The bookcase
is designed like a building's facade,
which is the image it projects.

The Buxton kitchen (2018, Bentley Home) is "an icon that grew out of the fertile encounter between the new Continental GT and Colombo's creative style.

"We focused on ensuring there was an identity that I could describe as almost genetic between the car and the designer kitchen. The forms are soft and captivating with fine materials and exclusive details like the sliding top that conceals all the technical fittings of the stovetop and the technological part connected to the mains."

The Harrow line (2016, Bentley Home) is ambitious and refined in its remarkable concern for detail, shaped outlines, and precious materials.

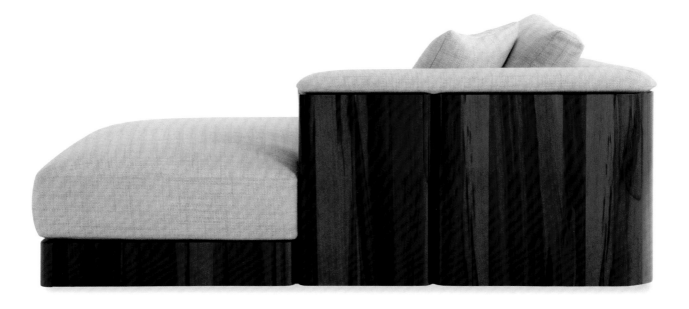

Tiverton (2020, Bentley Home) is a two-tone bed presented by the well-known carmaker. The upholstery can be interpreted in a variety of prized fabrics and leathers, enclosed at the sides by a sinuous curving headboard lined with a precious wood veneer. The headboard is also available embroidered with the iconic Bentley Home logo.

The Newent chair (2020) offers an exclusive insight into the Bentley Home universe. The excellence of all-Italian craftsmanship has made it possible to translate the silhouettes and codes of the British brand into domestic spaces. Organic, soft forms enclose the fine leathers and fabrics and the elegant curves of the Bentley world within a wooden shell, made even more iconic in the curving profile shaped by the latest generation production techniques. In this project, the search for stylistic renewal within the Bentley line is evident in the slender and less austere forms, very restrained and contemporary, aimed at a more international clientele not exclusively in the Far East.

A domestic architecture that stamps its character on its setting and adapts to every need. From mini to maxi, thanks to its modularity, Skyline (2019, Giorgetti) can be reconfigured repeatedly over time and equipped with accessories that also perform the function of armrests. Its advanced feature is the special reclining mechanism that enables the headrest to be adjusted for better relaxation.

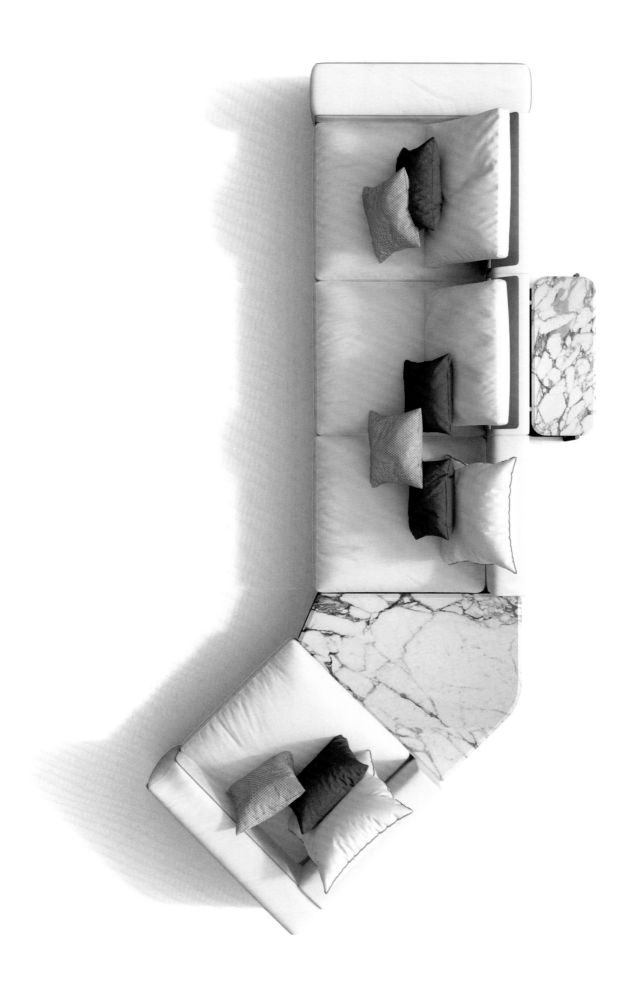

Domus (2020, Giorgetti) is a modular bookcase and cabinet line with built-in lighting, in wood, metal, glass, and leather. "Domus decrees a return to rigorous volumes, right angles and straight lines, the beauty of restrained forms." Modular and customizable, it renews the contemporary home interior.

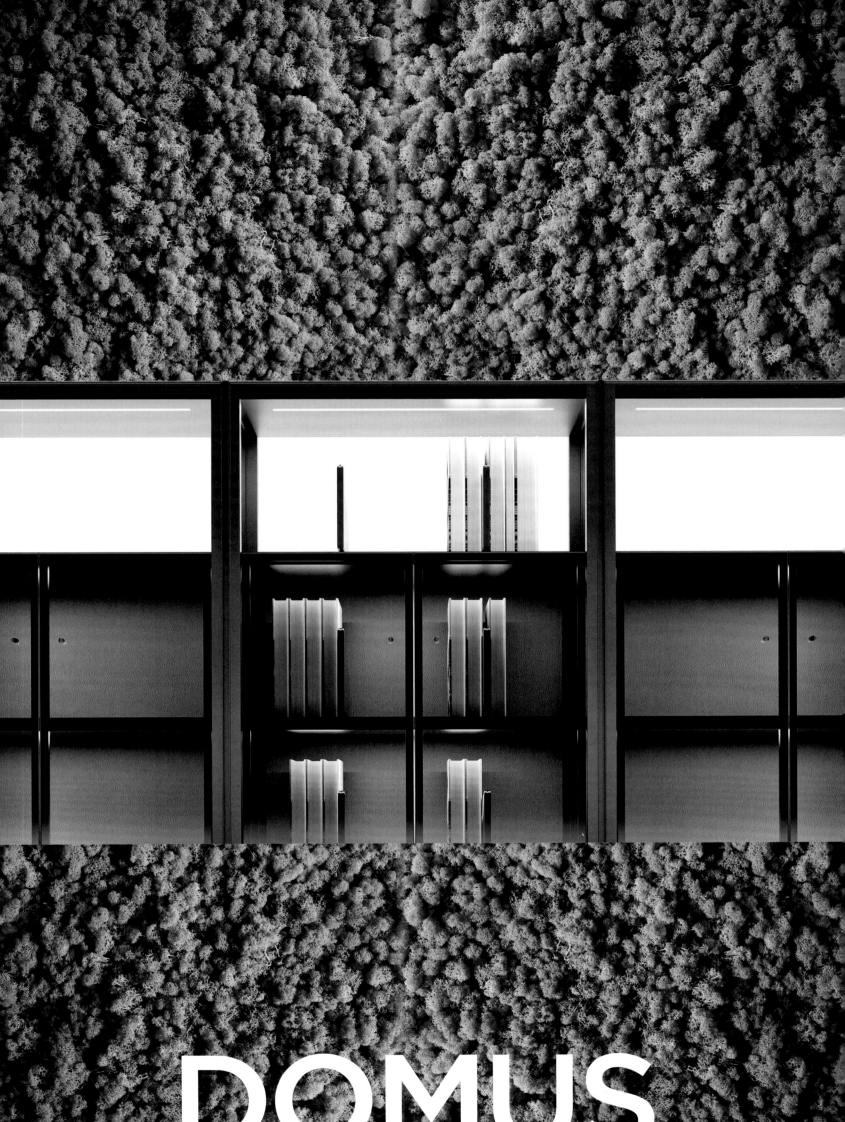

DOMUS

A system
that ensures
the extreme
personalization
of interiors with
a program of 100
different modules
diversified by
size, height,
and function.

Styal desk (2021, Bentley Home) is the high-end furnishing designed by Carlo Colombo in partnership with the Bentley Motors design team. In harmony with the seductive design of automobiles, the desk is a sequence of curves unfolding across the 10 feet (3 meters) of its wooden structure, exposed or faced with leather, with the cabinet elegantly positioned to give it balanced proportions. The top, faced with wood veneer with a gloss finish or leather, is marked along its entire length by a gunmetal insert—a graphic incision that accentuates its sculptural profile, dictating its lines and anticipating the curves at the ends.

2021

With sensuous lines
and poised forms and
composition, Bentley enters
the world of office furniture.

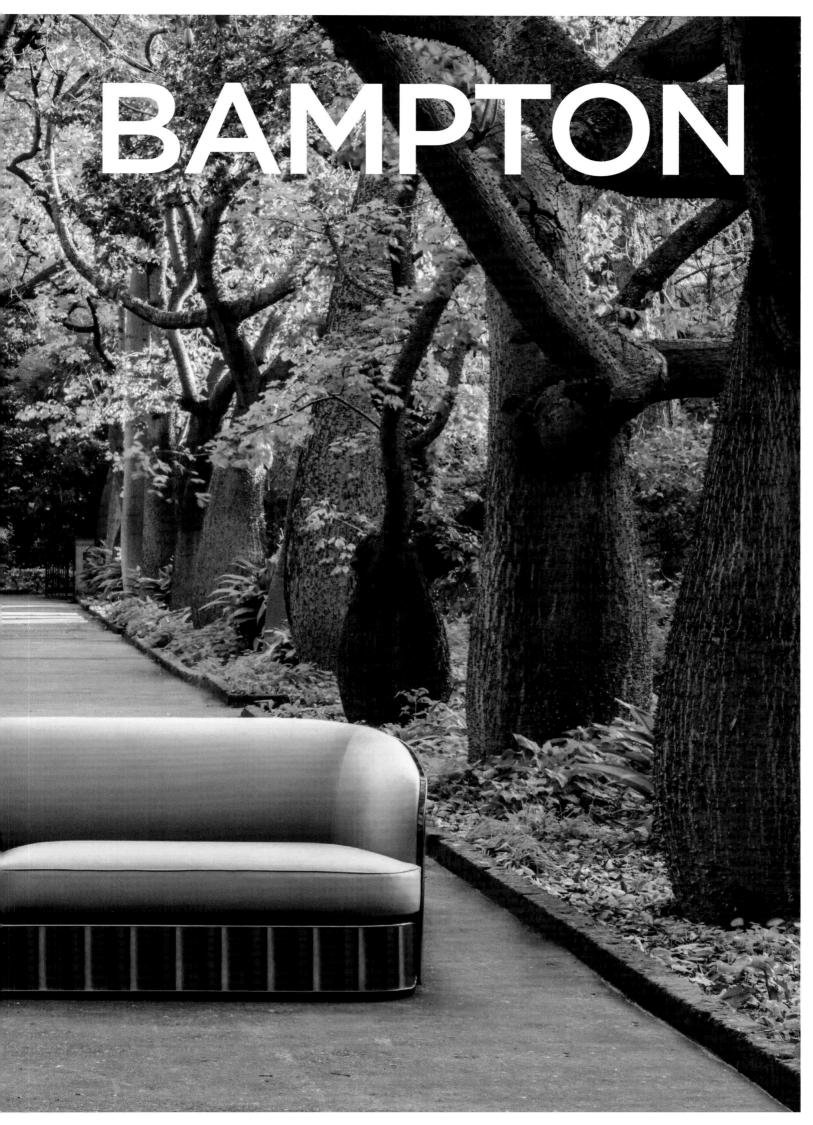

BAMPTON

Sofa with a design inspired by the dashboard of Bentley autos. The shell outlines a soft form with harmonious lines in which the back slopes seamlessly into the armrest.

Bampton (2020, Bentley Home) has a very full, welcoming seat with prized leather upholstery, which fits into the structure in original gloss-finish larch wood, its profile marked by a slender metal fillet.

ZOE

Zoe (2005, Rugiano) is a sculptural table with a cast
bronze base. The round tops are available in wood,
covered in leather, decorated or in marble.

Carlo Colombo with Vittorio Sgarbi sitting on the
784 armchair. The well-known art critic stressed
the suggestion that the iconic "throne" should be
produced in only nine copies as befits art multiples.

1990*2020

ART DESIGN

collection

"Being a collector means loving contemporary art, from pop to conceptual passing through a dreamy figurative art," but for Colombo it also means drawing on the evocative force and effortless creativity of art's experimental and rebellious universe. From works by Warhol or Rauschenberg, Schifano, or his favorite and magical Luigi Ontani, he derives the inspiration for composition, color, and forms, but he is even more inspired by the artworld in his conception of one-off design pieces, almost contemporary sculptures, presences that are space, light, and place.

These experiments have involved him over the last ten years, in line with a trend definitively sanctioned in 2000 by Design Miami Basel, the exclusive modern antiques and design festival devised by Ambra Medda to flank the more famous Swiss-American contemporary art fair. In this way, in the large parterre of Colombo's production, we find a range of seating with a markedly artistic and sculptural value, as in the case of the 2010 polyurethane Raspberry, or the mythical "gilded throne" 784 of 2016. These were a succession of notable works anticipated by the magnificent Ball in chromed steel of 2008, issued in a limited edition. These experiments with form, techniques, and materials, numbered or custom-made, join the already considerable output of pieces of industrial design devised for the most famous brands on the international scene.

"I was interested in getting out of the rut of industrial production and creating something exclusive."

The 784 is a contemporary throne made up of hundreds of gilded aluminum bars that make it as unique as a work of art. Poised between design and art, this galvanized aluminum seat inevitably becomes the centerpiece of every setting. Its gilding and massive presence evoke historic and exotic realms such as Egyptian and phantasmagoric environments that would have appealed to D'Annunzio or Mata Hari.

784

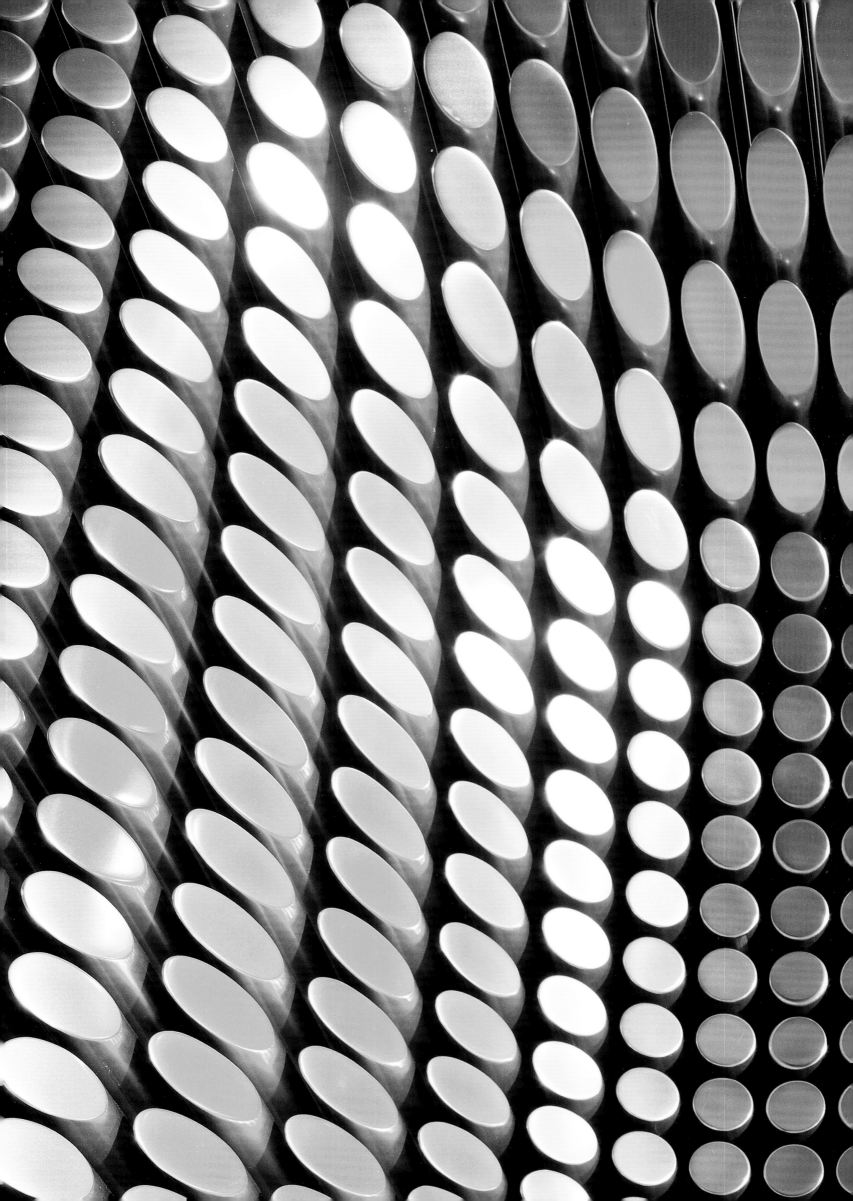

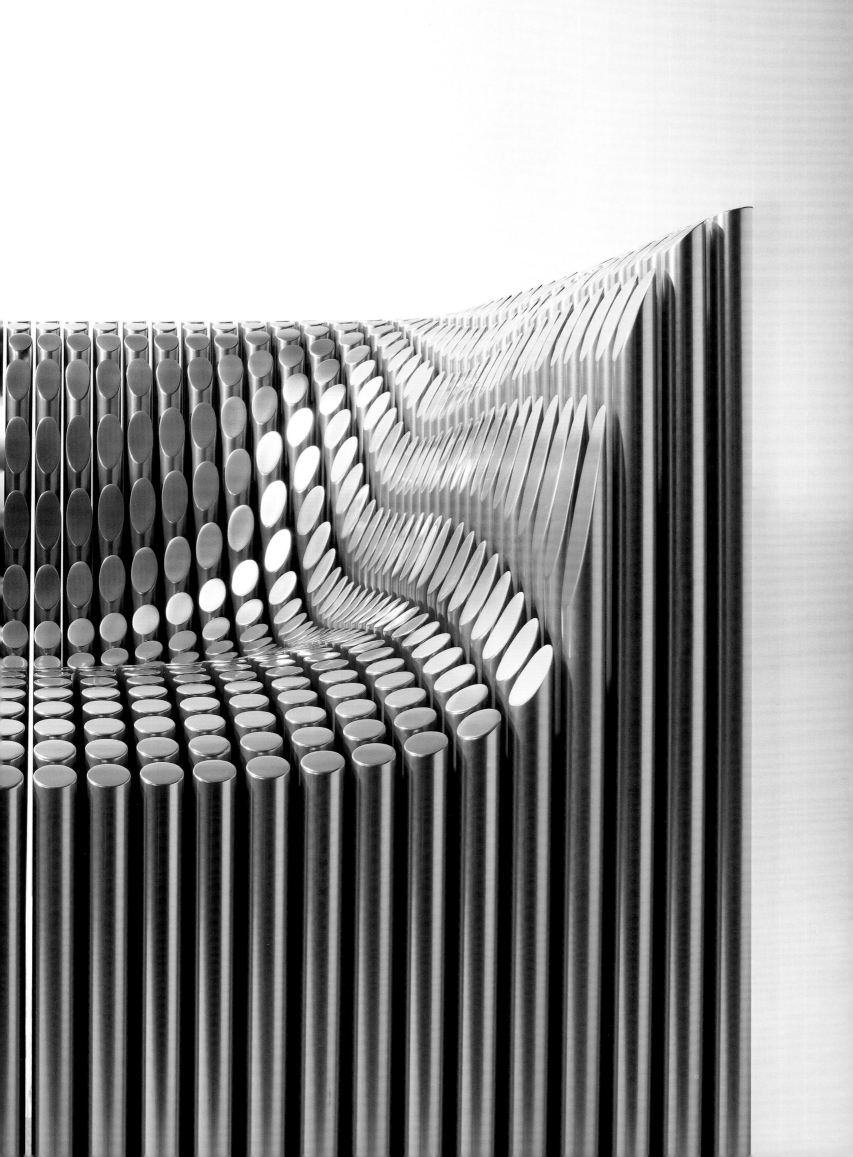

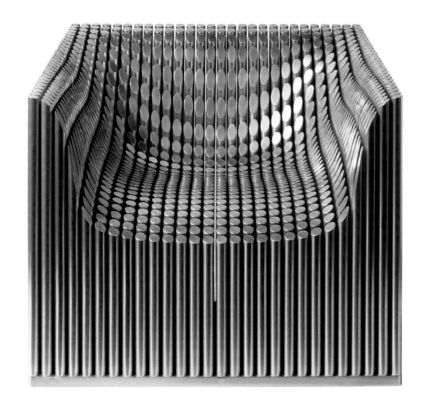

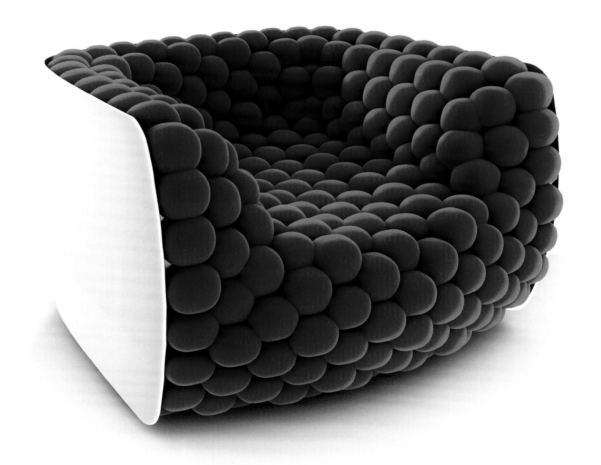

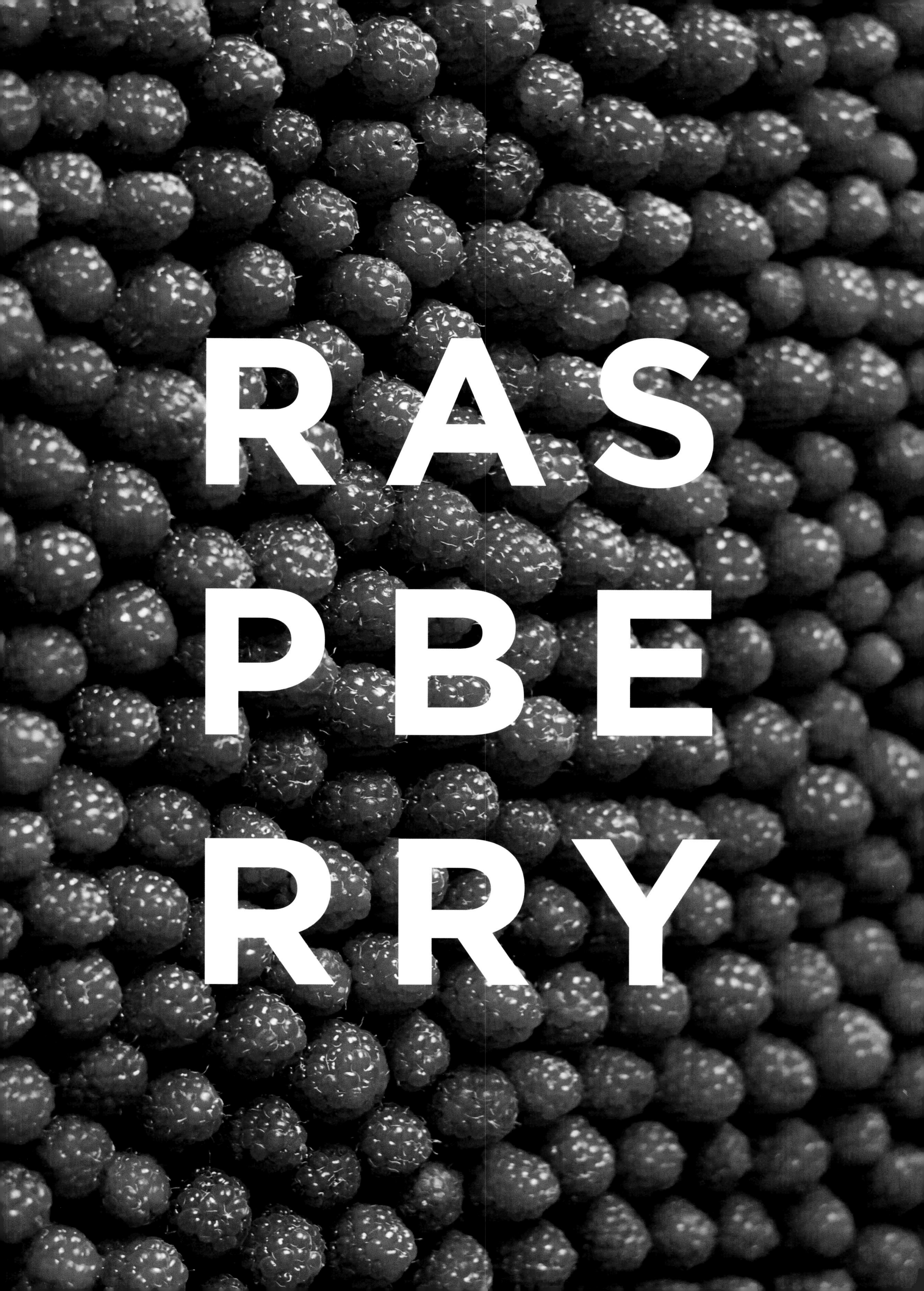
RAS
PBE
RRY

2010

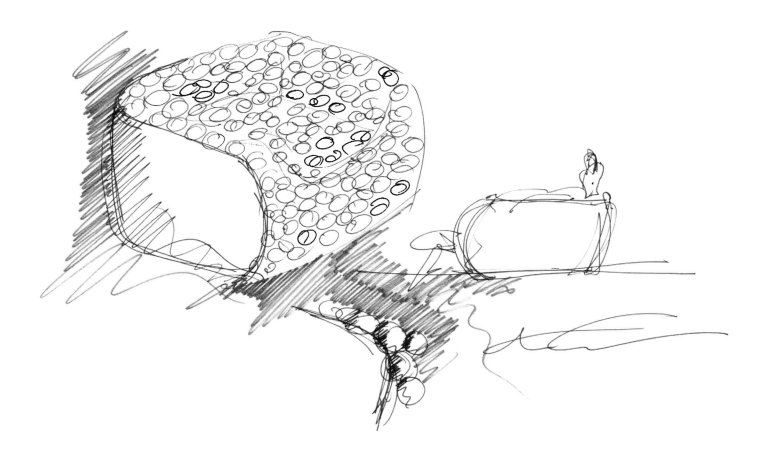

Rubbery spheres in polyurethane foam lined with technical fabric (232 of them) completely cover the seat and suggest the name of the Raspberry sculpture-armchair (2010, Carlo Colombo). The spheres are grafted onto a wooden structure covered with a scratch-resistant plastic shell, colored black or white or covered with a film to create a metal effect.

FOLIO

Folio (2021). An elegant sofa conceived as a one-off
piece within Carlo Colombo's art-design collection.
Fashioned in curved smoked liquidambar plywood,
this sofa recalls the thirties as well as certain
Futurist forms, while always conveying a timeless
elegance. It is one of those crossover objects that
span the sphere of design as well as art.

2021

Halfpipe (2021, Carlo Colombo). Curved tubes
fashion the silhouette of this armchair, revealing
the skeleton of the shell and highlighting its lines.

BALL

A veritable sculpture fashioned as a single spherical, polished steel casting modeled internally to welcome the human form.

The Ball armchair (2008, Carlo Colombo) was issued in a limited edition of 20, all numbered and signed. It is a contemporary object but also very rare. The exterior is smooth and polished, while the interior is articulated with ergonomic horizontal grooving. The resulting design is extremely refined, fresh, and capable of conveying the playful spirit by which it seeks to combine comfort and functionality. Despite the rigidity of the materials used, Ball conveys a feeling of softness and hospitality thanks to the human imprint that shapes the seat.

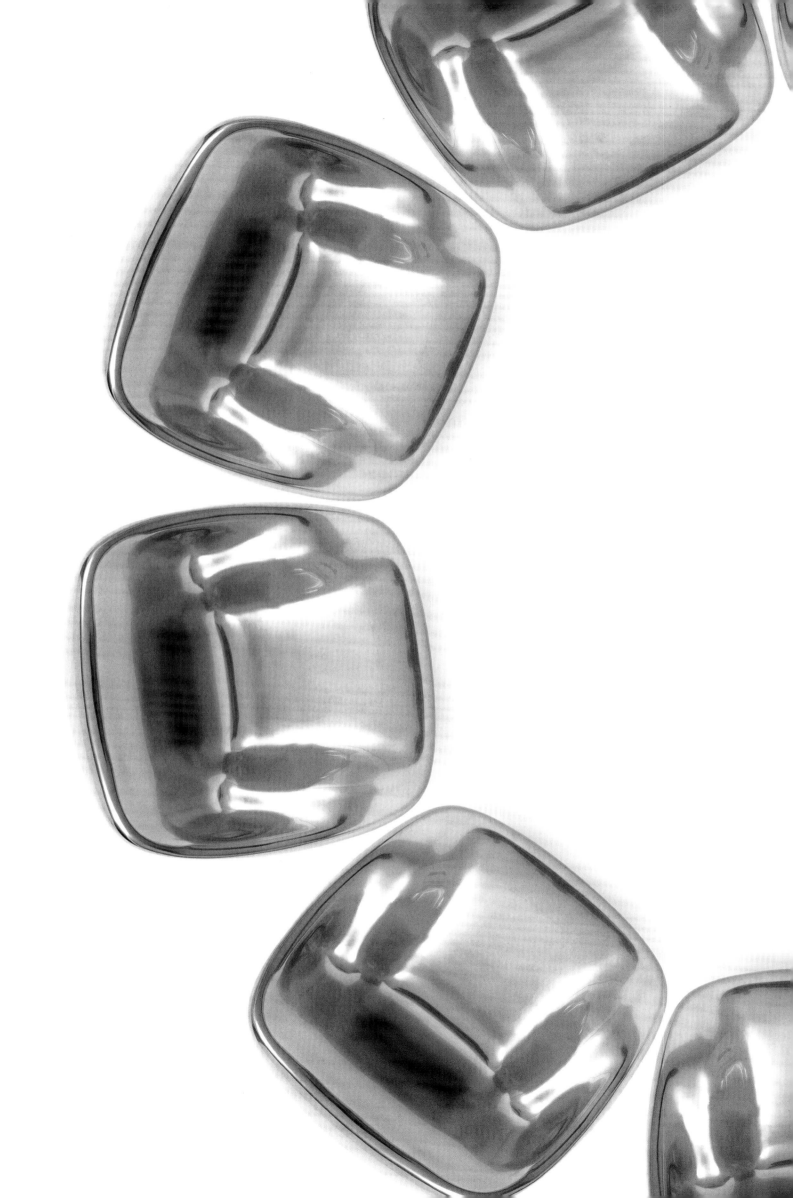

2021

Fold (2021, Carlo Colombo). The curved wooden plywood frame enfolds this sofa, creating
sinuous forms that fold back on themselves—almost like scrolls—defining symmetrical
and at the same time functional open spaces for storing newspapers and objects.

FOLD

Lobster (2021, Carlo Colombo) draws on the magnificent seventies in its fragmented silhouette and bright colors. This enveloping armchair with a polyurethane structure, upholstered in leather or fabric, is designed in two versions, high and low. The shape is reminiscent of the carapace of a lobster and this feature makes it welcoming, sculptural and, in the version with a chromed metal profile, even more exclusive. By right it belongs to that series of one-off pieces created by Colombo and poised between design and art.

LOBSTER

BULLFROG

Bullfrog (2022, Carlo Colombo), lively, refined, and versatile: the armchair
tastefully accents private and contract environments with his eloquent presence.
Extremely comfortable and softly enveloping, this armchair presents a cylindrical
back in a semicircle resting on a curvilinear metal structure, also used in the base.

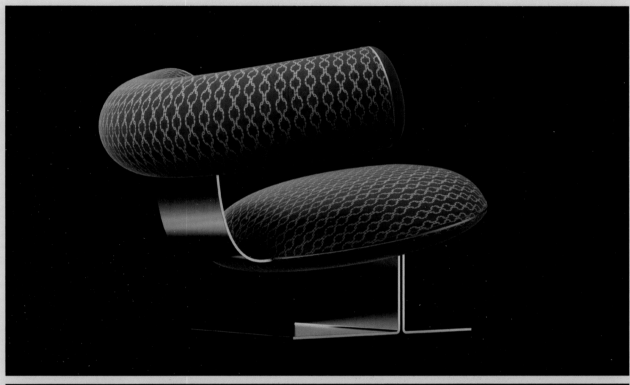

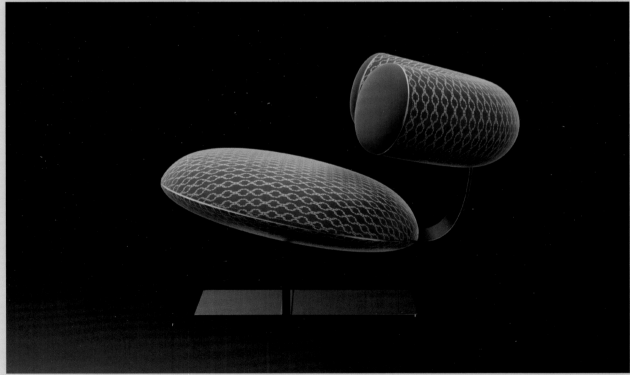

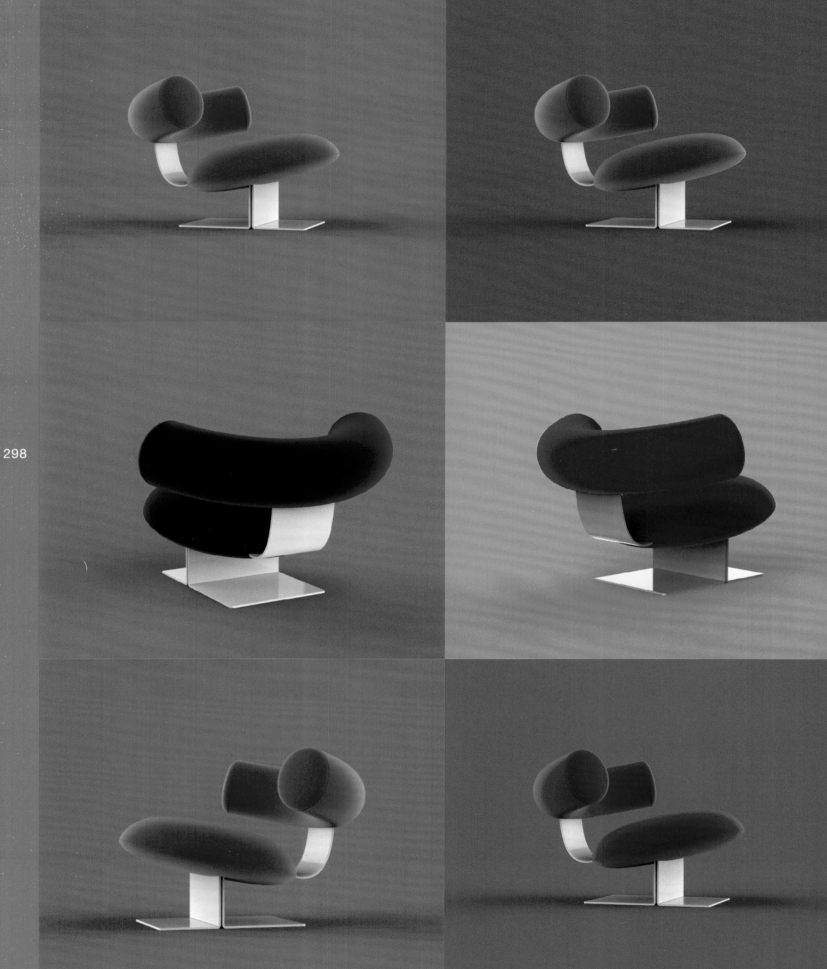

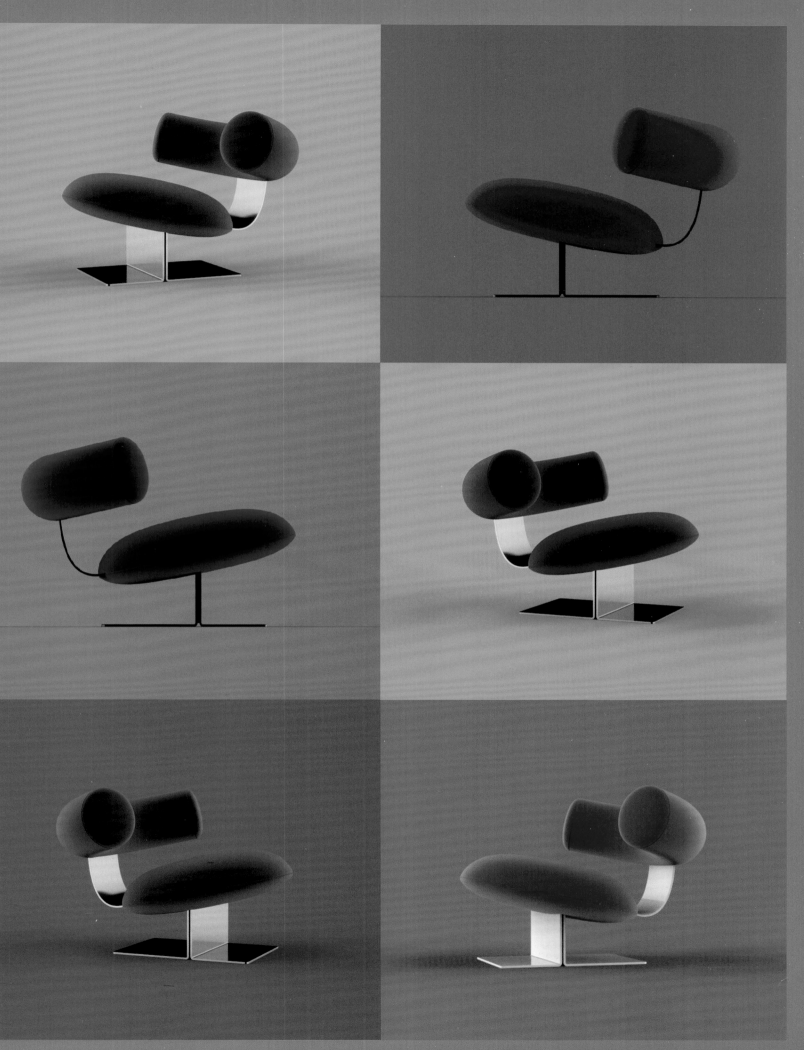

Carlo Colombo graduated in architecture from the Politecnico di Milano in 1993.
He began to work, dedicating himself, above all, to design and marketing of industrial products, graphics, and set-ups, collaborating with the best brands of Italian design such as Flexform, Poliform, Giorgetti, Cappellini, Antoniolupi, Artemide, Flou, Bentley Home, Bugatti Home, Trussardi Casa, Elie Saab Maison, Olivari, Faber, Sahrai, and Penta Light, to name a few. Since 2011 he has been teaching design at the University of Beijing. In 2013 he founded A++ architecture studio with Paolo Colombo in Lugano, which deals with interiors and large-scale projects all over the world, with studios in Lugano, Zurich, New York, Miami, and Dubai. His projects have been exhibited in Paris, at the Weserburg Museum of Modern Art in Bremen (1995), at the Museum of Decorative Arts in Cologne (1996), at the Milan Triennale (2016), and at MARCA, Museum of the Arts of Catanzaro (2017).

2004 Designer of the Year
2005 Elle Decor International Design Award
2008 Elle Decor International Design Award
2009 Good Design Award
2010 Elle Decor International Design Award
2011 Elle Decor International Design Award
2012 Red Dot Design Award
2014 Red Dot Design Award
2014 Interior Innovation Award
2014 London Design Awards
2014 Red Dot Design Award
2015 Red Dot Design Award
2015 iF Product Design Award
2016 100 Eccellenze Italiane
2016 Elle Decor International Design Award
2016 Presentation at Triennale di Milano 2016 con la 784
2016 IDA International Design Awards
2017 International Design Award, Los Angeles
2017 Knight title by the Italian Consulate in Switzerland
2018 APDC*IDA – Design Excellence Awards
2018 Interior Design Award
2019 Wallpaper* Design Award
2019 European Product Design Award
2019 The Executive Award - Designer of the Year
2021 Best of the Best 2021 by Robb Report
2021 Quirinale Contemporaneo
2022 Art Director in Master Contract Interior Design - Istituto Marangoni Milano

© 2021 Mondadori Libri S.p.A.
Distributed in English throughout the World
by Rizzoli International Publications Inc.
300 Park Avenue South
New York, NY 10010, USA

ISBN: 978-88-918290-6-1

2021 2022 2023 2024 / 10 9 8 7 6 5 4 3 2 1

First edition: April 2022

English translation: Richard Sadleir
Cover: Carlo Colombo
Graphic project: Carlo Colombo, Matteo Borriero
www.carlocolombo.com

This volume was printed at O.G.M. SpA
Via 1ª Strada, 87 - 35129 Padua
Printed in Italy

Visit us online:
Facebook.com/RizzoliNewYork
Twitter: @Rizzoli_Books
Instagram.com/RizzoliBooks
Pinterest.com/RizzoliBooks
Youtube.com/user/RizzoliNY
Issuu.com/Rizzoli